THEY WILL SEE HIS FACE

hen the angel showed me the river of the water of life, as clear as crystal, flowing from the throne of God and of the Lamb down the middle of the great street of the city. On each side of the river stood the tree of life, bearing twelve crops of fruit, yielding its fruit every month. And the leaves of the tree are for the healing of the nations. No longer will there be any curse. The throne of God and of the Lamb will be in the city, and His servants will serve Him. *They will see His face,* and His name will be on their foreheads. There will be no more night. They will not need the light of a lamp or the light of the sun, for the Lord God will give them light. And they will reign for ever and ever. (Revelation 22:1–5, emphasis added)

It is in the eternal worship, reflected in the Divine Service, that we see the face of God. Made holy through the body and blood of Christ, we have access to the Father by the Holy Spirit. We stand before Him as He reveals Himself in Word and Sacraments.

They Will See *His* Face

Worship and Healing

RICHARD C. EYER

CONCORDIA PUBLISHING HOUSE · SAINT LOUIS

To my children, John and Mary,
who will see His face!

Scripture taken from the HOLY BIBLE, NEW INTERNATIONAL VERSION®. NIV®. Copyright © 1973, 1978, 1984 by International Bible Society. Used by permission of Zondervan Publishing House. All rights reserved.

Copyright © 2002 by Richard C. Eyer
Published by Concordia Publishing House
3558 S. Jefferson Avenue, St. Louis, MO 63118-3968
1-800-325-3040 • www.cph.org
Manufactured in the United States of America

Library of Congress Cataloging-in-Publication Data

Eyer, Richard C., 1939–
  They will see His face : worship and healing / Richard C. Eyer.
    p. cm.
  ISBN 0-570-06771-5
1. Liturgics. 2. Healing—Religious aspects—Christianity. I. Title.
  BV178 .E96 2002
  264—dc21

                                                          2002008790

4 5 6 7 8 9 10 11 12 13   16 15 14 13 12 11 10 09 08 07

CONTENTS

PREFACE

When I was asked to write a book about Sunday morning public worship on "liturgy and healing," I accepted the invitation with eagerness. Having served as a hospital chaplain for 20 years, I frequently met people who in childhood had attended Sunday morning worship, but who in later years had either drifted away through mere neglect or had abandoned the church over some disagreement with the pastor or another parishioner. Some who had stopped attending were angry with God over something in life that did not turn out as they had hoped, while they at the same time felt guilty over their neglect of God in public worship. Most were reluctant, due to continued hurt feelings or embarrassment, to return to God in public worship. Drained by weariness from life's hardships, they often seemed to me as a lonely sailor drifting in a boat without sail or oars, who has given up all hope of returning to the mainland while at the same time longing for it. It is not that such drifters have stopped believing in God or even that they have stopped praying on occasion, but they have lost the meaning of worship and the conviction that worship is indeed a vital part of life with God the Father, Son, and Holy Spirit.

So I agreed to write this book about Sunday morning public worship and, more specifically, about the liturgy of Word and Sacraments. But I did not want to write a textbook on the liturgy. I simply wanted to write about the meaning of liturgy and public worship for those who want to know what worship on a Sunday morning has to do with their daily life. I believe it is possible to speak about things that are true for all people in a way that is personal, so I will write about how the liturgy has touched my life and the lives of those I have known. In this book I have tried to show something of my own experience of the healing that God gives in public worship through the liturgy of the Divine Service such as Christians have made use of for two millennia. I have chosen to write or sketch my thoughts only "after church," when the experience of worship and the healing that God brings was fresh on my mind. At times I made a brief note to myself during the service when some new insight struck me as I worshiped. These occasional notes also served as a basis for my personal meditation during the week.

I have chosen to write in a way that is personal because there are those who believe that if public worship doesn't speak to us personally, it isn't worth attending. However, I think it is a mistake to measure the worth of something merely according to one's own personal tastes. For example, I may not like to wear a hat in the winter, but I know from experience as I grow older and lose more hair that I am likely to regret it later if I don't. I wear a hat not because I feel like it, but because it is a good thing for me to do. In worship, some things may seem strange and even feel awkward until we come to understand the truth and benefit that result from doing things that way. It is important to remember that worship is not what we like to do, but what God has chosen to do for our benefit. Worship is primarily God's action in our lives through Word and Sacraments and only secondarily our action in response to that as prayer, praise, and thanksgiving. The attitude that makes the worshiper, rather than God, the judge of what is essential in worship risks missing what God is trying to give us.

I have been asked to make clear the connection between liturgy and healing. The healing that comes through the liturgy of Word and Sacraments is a healing of our self-centeredness, our guilt, our anxiety, our loneliness, our grief, and our physical and intellectual sicknesses. Liturgy is the form that worship has taken since God brought together a people for Himself under Moses. It is not merely form for its own sake, but it is form that conveys what God does to prepare us for and present us with the life support of His grace. The historic liturgy that Christians have used in worship since New Testament times and the early church has its roots in the Old Testament instructions to the ancient people of God that were given by God Himself. God has always revealed the where, the how, and the when of His work through what happens in the gathering of God's people at worship. The New Testament reveals the fulfillment of the Old Testament liturgy in Christ and invites every Spirit-filled believer to join with angels, archangels, and all the company of heaven in worshiping God as Father, Son, and Holy Spirit. In so doing, we find healing for the curse that sin and death have brought on us.

Christians need to be taught the meaning of the liturgy in every generation, not just once, but throughout a lifetime. By *liturgy* I mean the meaning, structure, and form our worship takes because of the content given us by God. The Divine Service is the highest form of liturgy because it conveys the real presence of Christ in the Lord's Supper. Worshiping God as He has called us to worship Him does not come naturally to us. By nature we worship self, not God. By nature we hide from God as did Adam and Eve in the Garden of Eden. Learning to worship God is an act of God's grace performed on us by the Holy Spirit. As parents and as members of the body of Christ, the church, we need to teach our children how to worship God and not leave it up to the tastes, trends, and inclinations of human nature. If God had not chosen to reveal Himself to us in Word and Sacraments, worship could be whatever we wanted it to be, but the Divine Service through which God works is His doing, not ours. We may update language, change musical settings, add our prayers for God's intervention, and work creatively to communicate the truth of God in ways each new generation can understand, but we dare not refashion Christian worship in our own image merely to suit our own likes and dislikes. The church is not a marketing firm appealing to the wants and wishes of the public to increase market share. Rather, we are a holy people living by God's Word, being prepared by the Holy Spirit to receive that which God gives us each Lord's Day in the Divine Service. It is our lifeline thrown out to us by God.

If worship were not God at work among us, the idea of "going to church" for any other reason would personally lead me to find other things to do on a Sunday morning. The cult of joggers and cyclists I pass on the way to church on Sunday morning might tempt me to join them as a way of pursuing the health I need for the toll that stress takes on me. There are many ways to "cope" with stress without Sunday morning worship, but there is only one place to find God at work in our lives the way He is in the liturgy of the Divine Service—offering healing at the core of life. Those who know what God is doing eagerly anticipate the chance to stand in God's presence each Sunday morning as He prepares them to receive His gifts of healing for the brokenness of their sinful lives.

Part of that brokenness sometimes causes me to attend worship on a Sunday morning for reasons other than why God desires me to attend. There are times when the only thing that carries my tired body from bed to pew is the thought of seeing friends and the social interaction that the fellowship of the congregation provides. But I am also aware that when I am focused on friends or the expectation of finding the church a friendly place to be, I am not as focused on God as I need to be and I miss the thing needed most. Unfortunately, worshiping God then becomes secondary to being with people I like. In contrast, I am best prepared to worship God when I take time to prepare myself on a Saturday evening to meet God the next morning, whether friends or friendliness can be found or not. God first, friends and a "friendly church" second!

The liturgy may seem uncomfortably formal to some. It is formal. Formality allows us to show reverence and awe before God. God chooses to come to us through form.

Formality lays aside the self in favor of something greater than our own discomfort. The formality of liturgy may seem strange to those who don't understand what is happening. On the other hand, Gene Edward Veith, in his book *The Spirituality of the Cross*,[1] describes how an unfamiliar liturgy introduced him to the awesomeness of worship and drew him into the Lutheran church. The formality of the liturgy seems to stand in bold contrast to the culture of informality surrounding us. Informality can be a rejection of the form God gives to life. But the liturgy of Christian worship is a mysterious thing, and mysteries are conveyed only through form, rituals, and things we may never fully be capable of understanding in this life. The liturgy of the Divine Service is the form, or formality, that unlocks the deeper meanings of our life with God. The liturgy uncovers needs we have that we would not otherwise recognize according to the norms of our contemporary culture. More important, the liturgy is the means by which God provides us with all we need in life to live courageously and faithfully in a fallen world, a world that will always be uncomfortable with the otherworldliness of the worship of the one true God. The liturgy opens a new world to us, God's world. In the liturgy of the Sacraments God invites us "to put off your old self, . . . to be made new in the attitude of your minds; and to put on the new self, created to be like God in true righteousness and holiness" (Ephesians 4:22–23). This begins in Baptism and carries on in Holy Communion. Liturgy is conversation with God on God's terms and by God's actions. In the liturgy we hear the healing Word God speaks, the Word on which our life depends. Through liturgy God invites us to discover

Him and our oneness with Him as a new creation with whom He is present to bless us with His healing gifts. "Therefore, since we are receiving a kingdom that cannot be shaken, let us be thankful, and so worship God acceptably with reverence and awe" (Hebrews 12:28).

1

THE GENERAL CONFESSION AND THE HEALING OF OUR GUILT

Guilt, resulting from the sin in our lives, is devastating to our relationships with one another as well as with God. The liturgy of the Divine Service begins by providing the healing we need with God and man in the General Confession before we begin our worship.

~

I f I ever allow myself to think that the need for confessing one's sins is an infrequent necessity, I need only think of my own marriage. I have been joyfully married for 35 years to a woman I dearly love. We have had our share of disagreements. This has not been a predominate characteristic of our relationship, but there have always been those regretful moments of disagreement in which each of us said things we ought not to have said and held anger against the other when it should have been left behind sooner. Fortunately, early in our marriage my wife taught me the practice of mutual confession and absolution. Shortly after we were married, at the conclusion of our first argument, I recall apologizing to my wife for being insensitive and unwilling to hear what she was saying, and as a result, she replied with considerable grace, "I forgive you." Her boldness in actually speaking those words made an impact on me, and I wondered if I was prepared to receive them, for it occurred to me that my repentance may not have been as genuine a response as it may have seemed. I was suddenly aware that I may have apologized merely to end the disagreeable experience rather than to actually admit I had done wrong or had sinned against her. That moment of her gracious forgiveness—remembered and repeated often over the years of our marriage—still amazes me. She was generous and accepting of me, a man who never seems to learn. I was not prepared for her absolution, and it caught me off guard.

It is one thing to admit your fault, even your sin, and quite another for someone to confirm your confession as necessary and to then repay it with forgiveness. I have become convinced that even our Confession of sins in the liturgy can be made with too little realization of what is about to follow as Absolution pronounced from God through the words of the pastor. The pronouncement of Absolution shakes the very foundations of our imperfect lives. Absolution both acknowledges that we do right to confess our sins and takes control of us so that we are renewed for a new beginning in Christ. Forgiveness proclaimed by God through the pastor opens the door to heaven and provides us a glimpse of Christ and a sure and certain hope of heaven. It is no fault of the liturgy that we do not always see this as we make Confession on a Sunday morning. It is the fault of our human weakness and our own inadequate preparation for worship. Unless we have previously spent time in daily personal devotions during the week, searching the soul, we will be unprepared for the impact of the General Confession in public worship.

We may carry our subconscious guilt into public worship but may have little awareness of the sin that gives rise to it and needs to be confessed in order to find healing for the soul. Learning to see one's sins begins with a willingness to allow it to happen and also a well-developed insight to recognize it when it does. If we are not willing to confess our sins, we merely bury the guilt deeper inside us, where it masquerades as irritability, insecurity, or depression. Guilt may wear a dozen masks and needs to be stripped away to uncover the sin behind it. A vague and generalized dis-ease of guilt makes it virtually impossible to appreciate the forgiveness that God offers for specific sins. We've all heard the voice of the guilt-ridden saying, "I know God forgives me, but I can't forgive myself." This may be true, but God can and does forgive sins when they are confessed to Him.

The General Confession may pass us by because we do not attend to our need for it. It is good when the pastor has a moment of silence before the Confession of sins so that the worshipers can collect their thoughts and prepare their heart. But where silence is provided in public worship without using it for such meditation, it may seem little more than an uncomfortably long interruption in the flow. We are not a people used to silence. It makes us uncomfortable, and we constantly fill it with music and noise that keeps our guilt and dis-ease at a distance. Too often the unease of the silence makes us impatient and we want to be done with liturgy that allows such discomfort. Some congregations eliminate the General Confession in worship altogether, claiming that it is unnecessary or too threatening to newcomers. But the fault is not with Confession; it is with the heart of the worshiper whose own nature resists renewal. When my wife and I confess our sins to each other, we speak an absolution to each other that is both humiliating and healing. We say in effect to each other, "I accept your confession as necessary to our relationship, and I speak my forgiveness to you as God has spoken it to me." Although this is one step removed from the pastor pronouncing Absolution "in the stead and by the command" of Christ, it is nevertheless husband and wife reminding each other of the reality and power of sin and grace in their life together. What we have both experienced many times in the liturgy, where Confession and Absolution prepare us to stand before God face-to-face, we now experience in the daily giving and receiving of married life. It is painfully corrective but always graciously renewing and genuinely awesome in relationship to God and to each other. Some years ago I received a letter from my daughter on the occasion of my 25th anniversary in the ministry saying, "I want to thank you for teaching me the meaning of confession and absolution in daily life." I should tell her that I learned it from her mother.

I remember vividly how my wife and I taught the practice of confession and absolution to our children. The occasion seemed to present itself around four o'clock in the afternoon, when the children seemed to concentrate their energies on testing the limits of our endurance as parents. On such occasions, when our nerves had been sufficiently frayed and some hard words had been spoken, it became clear to all that things were deteriorating. The only way to salvage relationships was to confess our sins to one another and seek one another's forgiveness. Doing so with children between the ages of three and seven required patience and a new humility on our part as parents, for confession of sins often had to begin with us for the children to learn to do the same. But after the first few times, it became a practice we all eagerly embraced. In fact, when things were not going well, it was often the children who said, "Can we have a powwow?" (That was the name we gave to what they later learned to call confession and absolution.) We would gather in the upstairs hallway (on neutral ground) near the bedroom to which one of the children had been "sentenced." Sitting in a circle, facing one another, each of us took turns civilly stating his or her case against the other. I had learned early in my teen years that my vivid anger toward God eventually brought me full circle to looking more honestly at myself. This same thing happened with the children if we gave them enough time. Eventually each of us discovered we were in need of confessing our own sins of self-pity, self-righteousness, and the sin of origin that had brought about the situation in which we found ourselves. So we let each child make his case against us, and we against him. We each tried to make our case truthfully and without the recriminations with which we started out. We were, as parents, trying to teach as well as absolve the children. Each person's legitimate complaint was heard and acknowledged. When each person had been heard and the problems clearly understood by all, before working out a solution, there came the moment for open, verbalized confession of sins and individual absolution. The children's confession usually included apology for tantrums, unreasonableness, rebellion, and the like. Our confession often included sins of impatience, insensitivity to their needs, and unreasonable reactions. Confession was followed by absolution, each forgiving the other for particular sins. In the end, solutions to the problems that had caused the conflict were easily resolved once confession and forgiveness had been shared. The session was usually followed by hugs and kisses and a generally good mood in celebration of our reconciliation.

But there were some times when we couldn't resolve the conflicts because one or more of us was still angry, unable or unwilling to let go of behavior or attitudes that were offensive. Sometimes all it took to break through this obstinacy was someone who was willing to initiate confession of wrongdoing as an encouragement for others to do the same. Sometimes we had to postpone the whole peace initiative until another time when everyone was more ready and willing to sit down and talk. None of this would have happened in our home had we not learned it early in public worship and, later in our lives, in the pastoral setting of private confession and absolution. Sunday after Sunday, what seemed an easy enough thing to do in church, namely confess our sins and receive Absolution from God, gradually took on a deep and practical significance in our daily home life as well.

There is a difference between confessing one's sins to

God in public worship, to a pastor in private Confession, and to a spouse or family member. Likewise, there is a difference between being forgiven by God and being forgiven by a spouse. When a husband confesses to his wife that he has wronged her, he hopes he will be forgiven by her, but unless he also confesses to God his wrongdoing, he has not yet enjoyed the Absolution of God. God's Absolution comes through the Word that God speaks and the Holy Communion in which God acts. This is why Paul urges Christians to make peace with those who have sinned against them before coming to the altar for God's forgiveness. Our refusal to confess sin is met with God's refusal of our entrance into His real presence in worship. We may occupy the pew, but to stand in God's real presence begins with the Confession of sins. It is the purpose of the General Confession to prepare us to stand spiritually in God's presence, as the psalmist says, "[with] clean hands and a pure heart" (Psalm 24:4). God is holy and we are His holy people, but we violate that holiness by our sins and need to be restored by Holy Absolution before we can worship God and rightly receive His gifts. It is one of the realities of being both sinner and saint at the same time.

If we are unable to think of specific sins to confess and there is nothing particularly troubling in our lives, the General Confession is an opportunity to confess, with Kierkegaard, that "in relationship to God we are always in the wrong,"[2] and that after receiving Absolution, in relationship to God we are always in the right. Public Confession and Absolution are public for a reason. Although we do not know one another's specific needs for Absolution, our common Confession of sins reminds us that we are all in this together. We are part of the one body of Christ. None of us can claim to be more in life than a redeemed sinner. We kneel before the altar alongside others to receive God's gifts of bread and wine, the body and blood of Christ, in acknowledgement of this and in reception of forgiveness. What other opportunity offers so great a healing of our lives? The closest thing to this outside the church is in the secular counselor's office, but even there confession of sins is seldom made and there is no absolution. As brothers and sisters in Christ we kneel side by side at the altar for Holy Communion as people reconciled with God and with one another. If we are at odds with one another in the congregation, we ought to be reconciled before we celebrate Communion in appearances together before the altar. We are not alone in the faith, but members of the one body of Christ. There is no room for people at the altar who are unwilling to work at reconciliation with other members of the body. Confession of sins, begun in public worship, needs to take on the day-to-day continuance in our relationships with one another. "Anyone who does not love his brother, whom he has seen, cannot love God, whom he has not seen" (1 John 4:20).

Through the practice of Confession and Absolution in the liturgy of public worship, we are made ready by God Himself to stand before Him. Children may be helped to grasp this, for example, in C. S. Lewis's Chronicles of Narnia. In that series the disagreeable young boy, Eustace, was turned into a disagreeable dragon, but is rescued by Aslan the Lion, the Christ figure in the book. The rescue occurs when Aslan tears the dragon skin off of Eustace piece by piece—a painful process, not unlike the agony of having to admit one's sins. When the scaly s[k]in has been removed, Aslan throws Eustace into the water for absolution. Then Eustace is able to rejoin the fellowship of the other children who followed Aslan. [3] When guilt is stripped away, the healing of the soul that takes place is a joy shared by human beings and angels alike. Stories such as this and the enactment of "powwows" help a child practice and appreciate the mystery of Confession and Absolution.

THE GENERAL CONFESSION

One version of the General Confession in the liturgy of the Divine Service invites us to make Confession as follows:

> Most merciful God, we confess that we are by nature sinful and unclean. We have sinned against You in thought, word, and deed, by what we have done and by what we have left undone. We have not loved You with our whole heart; we have not loved our neighbors as ourselves. We justly deserve Your present and eternal punishment. For the sake of Your Son, Jesus Christ, have mercy on us. Forgive us, renew us, and lead us, so that we may delight in Your will and walk in Your ways to the glory of Your holy name. Amen. [4]

In the words "by nature sinful and unclean" we are reminded again that "in relationship to God we are always in the wrong." We are all in need of having the dragon skin torn from us by Christ, the Lion of Judah. Acknowledging sin as "thought" as well as "deed," we are prevented from reveling in degrading imagination or from congratulating ourselves that at least we didn't act it out. In confessing as sin things we "have done and . . . left undone," we confess sins of commission and omission. It is not enough in the economy of God to avoid doing the wrong. It is also necessary to do the right thing when called upon to do so. The fact that we fail in both categories leads us before the altar to confess our sins. In admitting that we "have not loved [God] with our whole heart," we acknowledge both our lack of love for God and our halfhearted love for one another as those who are made in the image of God. Loving God is not just something we feel. It is something that we do with the right attitude. As children know down deep when they have done wrong and cry out to be called to account as proof of a parent's love, so we all know that living without the accountability required in public and private Confession of sins will in the end leave us desolate and uncertain of our relationship with God and with one another.

The public order of Confession therefore continues with the observation that we deserve "punishment" for our sins. But it is not a punishment we are entitled to inflict on ourselves or on one another. Those who make themselves miserable out of guilt for their sins are taking on themselves the prerogative of God. God does not call us either to inflict harm on ourselves or to give another person permission to punish us. It may occur in the secular realm that punishment for crimes is appropriate for Christians and non-Christians alike, but in the spiritual realm the only one entitled to inflict punishment is God. And God does inflict punishment, but only as a means of drawing closer to us. In Christ He takes the ultimate punishment for our sins on Himself. Any attempt to make restitution through self-inflicted harm adds to the list of sins we need to confess. Even self-pity as self-inflicted punishment is a wallowing in sin. There is nothing left to do when God removes our sin and takes our punishment on Himself in Christ but to receive it in faith and rejoice in it. Although it is easier to wallow in our sins, it requires faith to rejoice in forgiveness. It is not easy to let go of our need for punishment. But God is a God of grace and not of our destruction. Christ alone became the embodiment of sin for us and destroyed sin's power over us by destroying our sin in Himself through His death for us. Sin, the offense against God's holiness, has been dealt with on the cross, the depth of which is expressed in Jesus' words of abandonment by His Father, "Why have You forsaken Me?" (Mark 15:34). And so for all this, in the concluding words of the General Confession we plead, "Forgive us, renew us, and lead us, so that we may delight in Your will and walk in Your ways to the glory of Your holy name."[5] There is pain in our Confession, and there is pleasure in the Absolution that God gives. We leave behind our guilt, and we move on to the worship of God with "angels and archangels and all the company of heaven." Having been prepared to do so through Confession and Absolution, we sing in the Sanctus, "Holy, holy, holy Lord."[6] Without Confession and Absolution in the liturgy we could never stand before an almighty and holy God in worship. Without Confession and Absolution in public worship we could not return to our homes for another week of living faithfully in a fallen world. The General Confession in the liturgy lays out for us a way of life that leads to our continual daily healing. The proverb is played out, "He who conceals his sins does not prosper, but whoever confesses and renounces them finds mercy" (Proverbs 28:13). And with mercy comes healing.

PRIVATE CONFESSION AND ABSOLUTION

Unconfessed sin is a killer. The psalm says, "When I kept silent, my bones wasted away through my groaning all day long. . . . My strength was sapped as in the heat of summer" (Psalm 32:3–4). Perhaps one of the most devastating developments in recent years is the inability to recognize our sin as sin. Since the 1960s and the cultural revolution resulting in ethical relativism, the idea of sin as an objective reality has eroded in our culture. With the growing attitude that right and wrong are whatever each person decides they are, little is recognizable as sin to the individual. And yet, for all this newfound freedom to redefine sin as we do, we are still devastated by our sins. I recall overhearing a well-meaning but wrongheaded physician telling a patient in the hospital that she had no reason to feel guilty about what she had confessed to him because, he said, "We now know that guilt is not necessary. Everyone has to decide for himself what is right and wrong, and your good intentions nullify your guilt." Young people give themselves physically to one another as if sexuality had little to do with God and our lives together as His holy people. The old biblical word *fornication* has dropped out of use even in Christian congregations, but it is a word that helps us identify the sin of "sex outside of marriage" that eventually erodes commitment, trust, and love and leads to disease and death for an increasing number of people. Same-sex relationships, or as the biblical translation calls them, "indecent acts" (Romans 1:27), have become merely "an alternative lifestyle." Greed has become "accumulation of wealth" rather than "the love of money [as] a root of all kinds of evil" (1 Timothy 6:10). And so it continues, as

Christians make accommodation to the culturally acceptable messages around them. And yet we all suffer for it.
Sexually transmitted diseases, unredeemable indebted-
ness, the disappointment of attempting to find fulfillment
in things rather than in God—all increase the dis-ease and
the diseases of society.

One of the aims of pastoral counseling and the inclu-
sion of private Confession is to help us to learn to recognize our sins so that we can confess them, be rid of them,
and live in the relief that Absolution gives. Without Confession of sins and Absolution from God, healing cannot
come to our relationship with Him or with one another.
We may learn to respect religion or to tolerate one another
in our differences, but we will not embrace God or one
another as we do in the body of Christ when Confession
and Absolution are practiced in faith. Our worship, as well
as our daily living, must begin and end with the Confession of sins and the Absolution that God gives in His holy
Word, spoken by the pastor and by each of us to the other
in Christ's name. We learn this in the liturgy of public worship, where the Word of God is preached and the Sacraments, even the Sacrament included by Luther as the
Office of the Keys and Confession,[7] are made available.

Private, or individual, Confession and Absolution has
been in disarray for some generations. Whereas the
Roman Catholic Church encourages but no longer
requires private Confession for admission to the Lord's
Supper, the Lutheran church has begun to reemphasize
private Confession and Absolution after years of neglect.
In Lutheran circles, private Confession and Absolution are
also not required, but they are encouraged. Luther under-

stood their practice to be a vital part of pastoral care. Lutheran hymnals include an Order of Individual Confession and Absolution for which a parishioner may ask the pastor to meet privately and do specifically what is done more generally in the liturgy each Sunday morning. Private Confession is especially intended for those who are burdened by some particular sin or for those who need to be reassured more personally that God really has forgiven them. Confidentiality by the pastor is absolute. Sins have been taken away and no longer exist. In private Confession the parishioner is given time and opportunity to enumerate the particulars of his or her sin(s). If a parishioner comes with a general sense of guilt and asks for help in identifying its particulars, the pastor might take time to help the person explore the feeling of guilt and its causes. Generalized anxiety is sometimes caused by sins we have been unable to identify and admit even to ourselves, much less to God. In private Confession and Absolution the hand of God rests on us more specifically as a healing presence when the pastor makes the sign of the cross on us and assures us that our sins are forgiven. We are then invited to rise from our knees (the posture of Confession) and stand in newness of life (the posture of the forgiven life). Confession and Absolution are gifts of the heavenly Father that work in us the healing that no counseling or therapy can provide. Confession, also the work of the Holy Spirit within us, is the surgery God performs that removes the cancerous condition that kills. Absolution, the work of Jesus Christ, is the new life that gives us hope and a future.

DISCUSSION GUIDE

SUMMARY

The topic of Confession and Absolution is foundational to our preparation for standing before God in public worship. Those who do not know how to confess their sins cannot rightly worship God. It is in the public liturgy of the Divine Service that we learn how to benefit from Confession and forgiveness. In addition, it is through the liturgy that retains this "Office of the Keys and Confession,"[8] as Luther called it, that our children and their children after them learn how to confess and receive forgiveness in order to stand before God. In this discussion period the aim is to learn to appreciate the need for the General Confession in public worship as a preparation for standing before God and as a way of teaching succeeding generations this crucial doctrine and practice of the Christian faith.

GENERAL DISCUSSION

1. Allow a brief introductory discussion of the General Confession as it is printed in the liturgy of the Divine Service, asking members of the group to describe what it means to them personally. Talk also about the difficulties it might present, such as trying to meditate when holding small children.

2. Talk about the need for confession and absolution in the home. How does the liturgy of the General Confession in public worship teach us to practice this at home? Allow any willing members to share their experience of confession and absolution in the home, but do not let anyone use this as an opportunity to say things that might better be said only to a pastor in counseling.

3. The uniqueness of the General Confession in worship provides

an opportunity that has no rival in our culture. Without this model in the liturgy, Christians have no place to turn for their healing from the disease of guilt and sin. How do people deal with conflict and disagreements where this is not available? The one thing that a secular counselor (psychologist, psychiatrist, therapist) cannot deal with adequately in a counselee is guilt. How does the secular world attempt to deal with it? Do they? If not, where does it show up in their lives?

4. Discuss private Confession and Absolution with the pastor. Look at Luther's catechism section on Confession. How does the need for private confession differ from what happens in public worship in General Confession? When might a person make use of this opportunity?

Bible Study

Ephesians 4:26–27 seems to allow for anger without sin, although anger often leads to sin. But it need not. How might this apply to anger in the home?

Ephesians 5:21 speaks of submitting to one another out of reverence for Christ. How might this submission incorporate Confession and Absolution?

Ephesians 6:1–4 speaks to the relationship between parents and dependent children. What are some of the obstacles to teaching children confession and absolution? Is one of the obstacles a parent's inability to admit when he or she is wrong?

Galatians 6:1–5 speaks of bearing one another's burdens. How might helping another person face up to his or her sin be a way of bearing the burden with that person? What are some of the difficulties in confronting someone with sin in order to help that person confess the sin and find healing?

2

The Name of God
and the Healing
of Our Anxiety

Anxiety is common in the fast-paced world we live in today. It is hard to get outside of ourselves to find balance in life. Our anxieties find healing in the liturgy of the Divine Service, where we call on the name of God and are lifted out of ourselves and given a holy perspective on life that frees us from anxiety.

~

Sometimes in the daily routine of life I wonder where I am heading and what life will bring. It isn't often that I have time to think much about it, but every once in a while, when there is time and space away from the daily routine, I sometimes find myself feeling anxious about my life. I have wondered whether I will be able to manage a job, marriage, parenthood, retirement, aging, and my dying. Will my children be able to cope with today's world? What will I do for my parents as they age and need my help? A little something deep down inside me awakens, and I have a vague sense of inadequacy for meeting these challenges. In psychology this is called free-floating anxiety. Something at the bottom of life is stirring the pot, and we can't quite put a finger on it or decide what to do with it.

I am one of those people who sometimes wakes up suddenly in the morning with thoughts racing toward an assessment of the day's obligations. Perhaps it is conditioned by the habit of having served for 20 years as a hospital chaplain and needing to be on alert at a moment's notice in the middle of the night to deal with a patient's crisis. Some days, in the early waking moments of the morning, I find that I have to get out of bed to wake up enough to think clearly and bring into balance the frightening demands before me and the grace of God's comforting realities. This may not be everyone's experience of generalized anxiety, but all of us have some version of it that is characteristically ours. Anxiety increases unless we can get outside ourselves and focus on the bigger picture of reality that includes God and His help.

We live inside ourselves, overloaded with self-imposed expectations. So it is no surprise that anxiety is common and takes its toll on us physically, mentally, and spiritually. Unfortunately, most of us have a tendency to treat only the physical symptoms of our distress rather than the underlying condition that is the source of these anxieties. We devote a great deal of time, money, and energy to stress management through physical exercise and healthful diets, but we hurry through the day, neglecting the deeper spiritual healing for our anxieties. It would be foolish for me to think that physical exercise and diet are unimportant, for I too suffer from tension headaches, lower back pain, irritable bowel, and all the things common to humans. Exercise and healthful eating and drinking make it possible to bear the burden of these mortal bodies that conceal a deeper need for healing. We live in a society obsessed with physical health that seeks well-being through the practice of therapies ranging from sensible to bizarre. Even I must admit to occasionally practicing aroma therapy, although it is the aroma of a good cigar accompanied by a glass of wine that allows me to sit and relax at the end of a long day. Others seek help in relaxation techniques, Eastern meditation, or Western medication for relief of their stressed-out lives. But we need something more than a long walk to relieve the tension or the latest therapy to come to terms with ourselves, as helpful as these things may be in the physical management of stress.

Unfortunately, renewal of interest in spirituality in recent years is often little more than a desire for relief of stress rather than a longing for God. The experience of my morning awakening seems to me to be a parable of our times. The parable is this. When I lie in bed half awake and begin to get anxious, it is only when I awaken fully and get outside my own internalized vision of the world that I find relief. So it is with our lives in general. We must get outside ourselves to see God and to see the world around us as one that God governs with our healing in mind. If the solution to our anxiety is pursued only within the limits of our own physical, emotional, and mental well-being, we will miss the greater reality, the presence and healing of

God that are received by faith in Jesus Christ alone. Jesus does not merely offer peace of mind from the stress of the day. He offers healing of the diseased soul that destroys both our lives and our eternal peace. Trapped inside our own individual lives, we will continue to become anxious and our vision will become increasingly distorted. We need an awakening, an intervention from outside ourselves, that will deliver us from ourselves.

This is the function of the Divine Service in the Christian life: to be taken out of ourselves and into the life of God. At the core, the problem of our anxiety is the problem of our constantly drifting away from the center of our lives, which is God the Father, Son, and Holy Spirit. Under the pressures of daily living we wander and sometimes run to the edges of life, where we eventually come face-to-face with our own anxiety. This anxiety is a warning sign that we have drifted far. We begin grasping for a secure place to hang on that will prevent us from falling over the mind's edge into the abyss of despair. At those desperate moments it feels as though everything depends on us and we know we can't hold on much longer. Out of desperation we begin digging in for a foothold with greater tenacity only to find ourselves more helpless than we realized and losing control quickly. As we drift farther from God, we either become more desperate for solutions or more numbed to life. The numbness seals us off from God and the desperation frightens us. We tell ourselves all we need to do is try harder or its opposite, relax more. We try to discover some new technique or lifestyle that will resolve the tension. The farther we drift from God, the more we are doomed to our own failing resources. In the end this destroys us both physically and spiritually.

God's response to our drifting is dealt with in the liturgy of public worship, and He begins by giving us a password by which to enter into His presence. That password, given us in the Invocation, is His holy name of "Father, Son, and Holy Spirit." In the Invocation, in the Benediction, and when we speak or sing in praise saying, "Glory be to the Father and to the Son and to the Holy Spirit," we call on God to lift us out of ourselves and into His healing presence. There, our vision of life is broadened and the air becomes fresh once again. It is there, in the presence of God and lifted out of ourselves by God, that we find healing for all our anxieties, worries, and fears. And if we are willing, they can all be left behind so that we may return to our homes in peace.

No other name can unlock the door to healing that is beyond all human understanding for this life and the next. There are some other experiences that may help us understand the power of a name. A young man in love for the first time, infatuated with an attractive young woman, repeats her name to himself a thousand times a day and finds that it changes his life. Everything he does has her in mind. A young mother, having given birth to her firstborn, calls her child by its name for the first time with a hushed reverence that may overwhelm her. Her life will never be the same again. As human names have this power to transform us mentally, so the name of God has power to transform us spiritually. In speaking the name of God in public worship, in the liturgy, we enter into a deeper reality that existed before the world was made and that is impossible to find in the material world around us. The name of the Father, Son, and Holy Spirit opens the door to heaven for our spiritual nourishment and healing in worship.

One of the most privileged experiences I had as a hospital chaplain was to prepare the dying faithful to depart to this greater reality of eternity with our Lord. As part of these intimate moments I provided them with the heavenly food of Christ's body and blood, as the liturgy says, as "a foretaste of the feast to come."[9] As the day of their death drew near, I often thought of myself as walking them up to the door of heaven. The door of heaven would open for them, and it seemed to me as though in the sacredness of that moment I got a glimpse of heaven. There was of course no visual glimpse but an overwhelming sense of the holiness of that moment, and then I felt left behind with the paradox of sadness and joy. With St. Paul, as much as I want to live and not die—for we are created as earthly people—I felt left out and resentful of having to return to the mundane things of this life. Nevertheless, it is in the mundane things of life that we are called to live in faithful preparation for the greater life to come with our Lord. It was these privileged experiences, filled with paradoxical realities, that enabled me to continue to minister to the sick and dying in hospital chaplaincy all those years.

Similarly, in the Divine Service we are led up to the door of heaven weekly and given a taste of the holiness that awaits us in heaven. Here and now, in the celebration of the Lord's Supper, the Lord opens the door of heaven and comes down Himself to feed us the bread of life. Cleansed from our sins in the General Confession and enabled by Him to call on His holy name in the Invocation, we are joined with Him on earth in a way He provides as no other experience can. And our Lord leaves the door open to us for a few minutes in the distribution of His body and blood so that "with angels and archangels and with all the company of heaven"[10] we share in the worship of all the host of heaven. There are members of the congregation and visitors who may come and go quickly on a Sunday morning, not realizing what only the eyes of faith can see. They have other things to do that preoccupy them. Their priority is to get out of church quickly and back to the "real" world. But there are those who realize that the experience of the Divine Service is the real world at a glimpse, a door to heaven opened to us each week so that we do not lose heart and are sustained for this life until we walk through that doorway at our Lord's invitation for more than a glimpse. The Divine Service is not the fulfillment of all that God has in store for us, but it is enough to sustain us and to relieve the anxiety that arises from the fears of life and death. Worship is, for the moment, as C. S. Lewis describes in *The Magician's Nephew*, "the wood between the world," where time stands still and we are drawn up out of the pool of this life to enjoy the peace, solitude, and healing of this momentary world of heaven on earth for a time.[11]

The primary focal point of worship is the altar. Above it the cross draws our eyes to Christ's entrance into our lives for the healing of the nations. Because we are physical people, we need physical signs of God's presence. As we sing the praises of God in response to the verses spoken or chanted by the pastor, our eyes are drawn to the altar and to the cross in remembrance of Christ's death and in anticipation of the Lord's Supper where Christ will come down to feed us the benefits of His victorious death and resurrection. In our congregation the choir sings from the rear of the nave or behind us in the balcony. This obscure location is chosen so that the focal point of their music is not the performance of the choir itself, but the cross of Christ to whom the music of the choir is directed. Worshipers who turn to look back at the choir may miss the opportunity to meditate on the cross and its meaning. The choir, joining with angels and archangels and all the company of heaven, leads the voice of the congregation, encouraging our praises and inviting us to join the songs of eternity.

Everything we do from the moment we enter the sanctuary, the holy place, until we leave needs to focus our attention on what God is doing in and for us in the Divine Service. Surely there are brief greetings to be made to those who sit beside us, our children to be attended to throughout the service (sitting up front helps the children to learn to focus as well), and there are pages to mark in the hymnal or bulletin inserts to have ready, but a minimum of attention to distractions will prepare us to experience God's presence among us. God does not come as one more thing in what some may see as an otherwise entertaining selection of hymns and performances (worship is not intended to be an entertaining performance), but as the primary thing in the Divine Service.

There was a time in my life when many liturgical actions made me uncomfortable, but over the years I have learned to make the sign of the cross, imperceptibly in public and openly in public worship, on the forehead and on the heart as was done in my Baptism, naming God as

Father, Son, and Holy Spirit in my life. In God's touching us with the sign of the cross through the hands of the pastor in Baptism, God has placed His name on us, claiming us as His own. We have been branded for life. Our Baptism is always valid regardless of our unfaithfulness, and we can be called back to it. Consequently, in the invitation to name God's holy name in public worship, we are claimed again by God, who frees us from our self-absorbing anxieties. Although making the sign of the cross with God's name can be done carelessly and without much thought, it is good to think again about what it means to make the sign of the cross. God is actually doing something by placing His name upon us in the liturgy of Baptism and each week in public worship. Nothing that God gives us in the liturgy of public worship is meaningless. It is only we who, in ignorance and in the tendency to distance ourselves from Him, become distracted by anxieties and oblivious to what God is doing in worship.

C. S. Lewis once said that the benefit of the repetition of the historic liturgy each week is that it disciplines us to pay attention to God and not be distracted by the newness of weekly changes in the form of worship. Lewis wrote in *Letters to Malcolm: Chiefly on Prayer*:

> The majority . . . don't go to service to be entertained. They go to use the service, or, if you prefer, to enact it. Every service is a structure of acts and words through which we receive a sacrament, or repent, or supplicate, or adore. And it enables us to do these things best—if you like, it "works" best—when, through long familiarity, we don't have to think about it. As long as you notice, and have to count, the steps, you are not yet dancing but only learning the dance. A good shoe is a

shoe you don't notice. Good reading becomes possible when you need not consciously think about eyes, or light, or print, or spelling. The perfect church service would be one we are almost unaware of; our attention would have been on God. [12]

If our worship is to be an experience of God's presence on earth, then we need to discipline ourselves to be receptive to that presence. It may be difficult for us to realize that the Divine Service is the door through which God enters our lives each week, but that may be because we are captive to the ever-changing cultural expectation of being entertained by onstage events and the television screen. We are not self-disciplined by nature to perceive God really coming to us in the liturgy of public worship. For some time now, Christians have followed the world's example of self-indulgence, reinventing worship to make it what we want it to be. Ours is a time in history in which we are obsessed with *self*. We value self-determination, self-fulfillment, and self-gratification more than the self-sacrifice of Christ for us and our salvation. Worship increasingly has become a public-relations experience, selling itself as satisfying our desire for friendships in this anxious world, rather than the need for fellowship with God. Friendship is not the same as fellowship. Friendship can grow out of fellowship, but fellowship with brothers and sisters in Christ may or may not develop into sustaining friendships. We may find friends elsewhere, even those with whom we are not in fellowship. This, in part, is what it means to be a neighbor to those in need of us and perhaps even we of them. To be friendly before and after worship is good, but to have fellowship during worship, we must be attentive to what God is doing.

From the beginning of time, God has chosen to reveal Himself to humankind on His terms, not on ours. This is because we must know Him as objectively real and not merely as a virtual reality created in the image of our own likes and dislikes. It is not our prerogative to attempt to create new techniques for God to make Himself known to us. Nor should we mistake our loss of delight in the Divine Service as the fault of the Divine Service. Ours is to respond in faithfulness to where God tells us He is to be found. From ancient times to the present, from Moses and the people of God who worshiped in tent and temple to we who gather in churches, God's presence has been made known in worship. God chooses to reveal Himself in the worshiping assembly. For us, people of the New Testament, our standing in God's presence begins with Holy Baptism, continues with Holy Absolution, and reaches its fulfillment in Holy Communion.

In preparation for worship it is always good to read the Scripture lessons appointed for the Sunday to come, perhaps on Saturday evening. In preparation for standing before a holy God it is also important to take time to examine our sinful lives during the past week and recognize our need for God's grace and mercy once again as we come before Him. Sin, arising out of problems of daily living, may present itself as generalized anxiety linked to a troubled marriage, a failing career, problems with relatives, or the loss of loved ones in death. We need to be where God makes His presence known and where healing takes place, in the worshiping assembly. God is the center of our lives, and worship is where that center is found. Saturday preparation is time to slow down the week's pace in order to think about our need for God and how God meets that need. Worship is where two worlds meet. It is the place where God comes down to earth to open the heavens to us. In the presence of God we enter a reality that cannot be known by the human mind without Him. The words of the liturgy tell us who He is and where He can be found. This God has a name that tells us not only who He is but who we are in relationship to Him and to one another. In the Invocation we call Him God the Father, Son, and Holy Spirit. If He is our holy Father, we are His holy sons and daughters. If He is the holy Son of God, then we are His holy brothers and sisters. If He is the Holy Spirit, then we are the holy ones in whom He lives. The name of God is more than a name; it is who He is and who we are. It is our return to the healing that God gives.

DISCUSSION GUIDE

SUMMARY

All of us get so caught up in ourselves that we can't see our own world objectively. We need to get outside ourselves to find our balance again. This healing perspective is found in God in the experience of the Divine Service, as we call on His name. In public worship we are invited by God to get outside ourselves and enter into the presence of God. When I speak my own name, I am focused on myself; when I speak the name of the Father, Son, and Holy Spirit in faith, the focus is on God. This divine perspective provides us with a place in our weekly living where we can let go of our anxieties and find renewal with God. There, through Word and Sacraments, God feeds us with His healing presence.

GENERAL DISCUSSION

1. Lead a general discussion on the topic of anxiety. Is it more than worry about something?

2. Are we as a society living with more anxiety than we did a decade ago? Why or why not?

3. What are people anxious about today? How does this anxiety show itself on a societal level?

4. Sometimes Christian motivational speakers promise that people will find relief from anxieties by taking charge of their lives by following certain spiritual principles. How does this Law-oriented approach differ from the Gospel-oriented approach of the Divine Service?

BIBLE STUDY

Matthew 11:28–30 speaks of coming to Jesus for rest. What is meant by *rest* here, and how might this rest be found in the Divine Service?

Luke 24:28–31 describes the presence among the Emmaus disciples "in the breaking of bread." The text says, "their eyes were opened and they recognized Him" (v. 31). Talk about what it means for our eyes to be opened and to recognize Jesus when we participate in the Lord's Supper.

Colossians 3:1–4 urges us, "Since, then, you have been raised with Christ, set your hearts on things above, where Christ is seated at the right hand of God" (v. 1). What does this mean for our worship? How, according to this text, in relationship to anxiety, do we die and hide with God in Christ?

Luke 2:29–32 describes Simeon's experience, "my eyes have seen Your salvation, which You have prepared in the sight of all people" (vv. 31–32). How do we "see" God in the Divine Service each week?

–3–

LITURGICAL PRAYER
AND THE HEALING
OF OUR LONELINESS

*Loneliness finds healing in the liturgy of the Divine Ser-
vice through liturgical prayer, which helps us keep our
balance between being with others and being alone. In
this healing, loneliness is replaced with solitude when
among people or alone.*

~

Being alone can be experienced either as loneliness
or as solitude. Loneliness is painful; solitude is
peaceful. Loneliness cries out for healing through
our relationship with God and the fellowship of believers.
Solitude is the comfortable aloneness of being at peace
with oneself in the presence of God. Solitude leads to cre-
ativity and renewal of vocation. Solitude does not require
healing—it delights in life as the gift of God. Although
many people experience loneliness, fewer people receive
the gift of solitude. Loneliness drives out solitude, and

solitude drives out loneliness. Loneliness is characteristic of living in a fallen world. It can be the result of self-imposed isolation due to our own bitterness and resentment. It can also be the painful, transitional experience of grief due to the losses in our life, the loss of a loved one through a death or divorce, the loss of opportunity to do what we have always enjoyed doing most, or simply the loss of youth and the unrelenting experience of aging that leads to a loss of vitality and physical health itself. Where loneliness is the result of self-imposed isolation due to bitterness and resentment, healing depends on finding forgiveness and a renewal of faith. Where loneliness is the result of grief and loss, healing depends on the spiritual care and fellowship with others who share faith in Jesus Christ. Loneliness cries out for the solitude that comes from a maturing faith. Solitude is found in fellowship with God and the worshiping community, where we are fed the Gospel in Word and Sacraments by God Himself.

Stirrings of a vivid, personal faith began for me as I entered the typically turbulent teenage years. As varieties of people have observed from Aristotle to Luther, it is in affliction or the bittersweet turbulence of life that we have opportunity to grow. Teenage years provide plenty of both as we try to discover who we are and what life holds for us. Having found identity and security in our parents' world, in adolescence we set out to find our own identity and purpose in life. This occurs, in part, through interaction with our peers, who are also trying to do the same. The challenge is in finding acceptance among peers while at the same time establishing an independence from them. By God's grace, having worshiped within the community of faith since early childhood, it was by faith that I learned to cope with life's adolescent turbulence and discovered the rare moments of a God-given solitude. I was not alone in this. More than a thousand years ago Augustine, whose years were marked by both turbulence and solitude, wrote, "Our hearts are restless till they rest in Thee."[13] Augustine knew the paradox of life in a fallen world:

> And sometimes You [Lord] cause me to enter into an extraordinary depth of feeling marked by a strange sweetness. If it were brought to perfection in me, it would be an experience quite beyond anything in this life. But I fall back into my usual ways under my miserable burdens.[14]

Walking home from school, I would sometimes take a path through an isolated wooded area that offered relief from the noises and nuisances of adolescent life. There, moved by sunlight filtering through the birch trees as if heaven itself was shining down on earth, I knelt to pray. The gentle wind in the leaves sounded to me like the "gentle whisper" of God that spoke to Elijah (1 Kings 19:12). There was, of course, no voice in those moments except that of my own in prayer. Such times were private and personal, and I guarded them as my secret for years. It seemed to me that telling anyone about that place or my experience would have desecrated it. We need such moments of solitude for mediation and prayers.

In contrast to these unplanned, occasional solitary moments, I also prayed each week with others in church on Sunday morning. I regularly attended worship services with my mother and in later years was joined by my father. But as a young man in search of himself, I seldom found the same awesome experience in liturgical prayer that I had found in private prayer. Apparently I was not alone in this. Throughout my ministry as hospital chaplain, I met people who said they believed in God in a very personal way but declined to attend public worship. They had created their own world of spirituality that provided them with the personal satisfaction that seemed to be missing in public worship. I think there may be many people who pray to God in private but who do not attend public worship because they find little meaning in it. Although as a child I did attend public worship regularly in spite of my occasional impatience with it, I do understanding the disappointment of those who don't. What happens in the deeply personal moments with God in solitude is not often experienced in the same way in public worship. But the problem is that we make a false comparison. The two are not meant to be experienced as the same thing. The problem lies in our misguided expectations and lack of awareness of what is available in public worship that is not available in moments of solitude. In private prayer we are left to ourselves with God. That aloneness can and must, to some degree, focus on ourselves. At worst, we can become preoccupied with self-interests and be demanding of God. In public worship, meditation and prayer is guided not by us, but by the presence of the kingdom of God among us as God's people gather to receive what God chooses to give even without our asking. But we do ask, as one body in Christ. It took me years to realize the meaning and experience of public prayer in worship, which I now value as a vital and indispensable part of my prayer life. It is for good reason that the writer of Hebrews urges, "Let us consider how we may spur one another on toward love and good deeds. Let us not give up meeting together, as some are in the habit of doing . . . and all the more as you see the Day approaching" (Hebrews 10:24–25).

As much as we need daily times of private prayer, when private prayer is not balanced by prayers among the community at worship, our private prayer always risks deteriorating into our misreading of the faith, other people, and the whole of life. We begin to see the world through the lens of our own eyes and not the eyes of God. In my college years I would sometimes decline an invitation to join friends socially on a Friday night so I could spend time alone with God, sorting out the things that were troubling me at that time in my life. Not knowing then the resources of liturgical prayer for personal devotional use, I found myself developing a style of my own, unfortunately shaped by my own emotion and feel-good piety. As a college student I was very idealistic on the one hand and critically introspective on the other. Although introspection can lead to constructive insight, by its very nature it also limits thinking to our own thoughts, thoughts untouched by outside influence of the body of Christ. Anyone who is conscientious about his or her faith may be tempted to keep it that way and protect it from any outside influence. Any attempt by others to draw us into a greater form of piety such as public worship may seem more an obstacle than a gift to be received. It was only a few years later in college, when my faith suffered severe trials, that I turned to my pastor and learned from him the meaning of worship in the body of Christ at prayer on a Sunday morning.

In private we are in danger of inventing our own version of the Christian life and of protecting it against interference, even unknowingly against God. The popularity of meditation techniques in our culture appeals to the desire to block out the world around us and enter more deeply into the self. Christian prayer does not enter into the self but consists in a cry for the Holy Spirit to lift us out of ourselves. This is what prayer in public worship also does. This is why the General Prayer, the short, pithy Collects, and other "written prayers" seem so uncomfortable and impersonal at times. They are not our own words or thoughts, but that is precisely what makes them important for us to use. They need to absorb us into the prayers of God's people at worship. Public prayer, like public worship itself, does not aim at meeting our personal felt needs. Public prayer aims at calling the unfelt needs to our attention and pointing us to God for their fulfillment. Faith expressed either in private prayer or as corporate in-public worship ought not deteriorate into feel-good self-indulgence, which is not to say that feeling good in prayer is wrong. Augustine recognized the danger of the senses over against the Word: "When it happens to me that the music moves me more than the subject of the song, I confess myself to commit a sin. . . . I would prefer not to have heard the singer."[15]

Public worship at prayer teaches us to experience the connection that gives objectivity to our faith. The liturgy is where God shapes our personal prayer so that He can respond to us in a way we come to recognize as His voice and not ours. If our prayers are not shaped by more than our own wants and intentions, we risk asking for the wrong things in the wrong spirit and receiving the wrong answers. In public worship God teaches us to pray by helping us to pray in His own words, with others. This is part of getting us outside ourselves where God can come to us in the uniqueness of the Divine Service to give us things we cannot receive in solitude. God speaks to us through the liturgy of Word and Sacraments in public worship, and we respond to Him, shaped by what He has said to us. We are assured then that what we hear from God is not the sound of our own inner voice, but the Word of God spoken into our ears, from outside ourselves, in the liturgy. It is not the same as private prayer, where we speak and await God's answer. In private prayer we commend all to God and say, "Amen." In the public liturgy we pray and God answers immediately by serving us. In private prayer we are always tempted to answer for God, but at public prayer in worship God answers by His Word—spoken, sung, and received in the body and blood of Christ. If private prayer is talking *to* God, then liturgical worship is constant conversation *with* God.

The invitation to prayer comes immediately at the beginning of the Divine Service when we are invited, "In peace let us pray to the Lord."[16] Most complaints about the liturgy, from people culturally conditioned to change, are that it becomes repetitious week after week. There is no doubt that repetition can dull the senses if we allow it. Even a husband telling his wife, "I love you!" can become little more than the recitation of a formula without serious thought, but hopefully he does not stop saying, "I love you!" He thinks about the words and their intent and pays attention to what he is saying so that it has honest conviction the next time he says it. Once we have allowed our-selves to assume that the problem is with the liturgy and not with us, those parts of the liturgy that are the same every week begin to become for us mere "fillers" taking up time and space between hymns, lessons, sermon, and Holy Communion. It would be like a dulled "love" between husband and wife that merely takes up time and endures the passing years.

I recall a course I had in my first year of college. The course was a general humanities course that covered everything from history to art, architecture, literature, and an unending list of names and places and events that seemed as irrelevant as anything could be to an 18-year-old wanting to experience the waiting social opportunities that college life offered. Nearly all of us complained about how the course was taught. In every class session we were given page after page of facts to be memorized and were tested on it the next class period. It seemed little more than "vain repetitions." Some of us, determined to make the best of it, got together each evening and made up ways to remember all the seemingly unrelated facts, attaching them to attributes of the professor, whimsical alliteration, nonsensical rhyme, or anything else we could to make it at least palatable. Some years after college I began to realize that we had been given an important framework for understanding the broader picture of our civilization. Seemingly unrelated facts were, in fact, essential pieces of a puzzle that made it possible to complete the larger picture of life's matrix. What once seemed meaningless, rote learning soon became the means to making sense of life's learnings and meanings.

Something like this happens when we learn the liturgy through repetition as children. The young child can easily learn the language of liturgy simply because of a new challenge of learning and is then more willing to participate in the prayers and liturgy of the church. My own children learned hymns in Latin and Greek around our dinner table by the time they were five years old because we sang them as part of our family devotions. If given the chance to participate in public worship—of course sitting up front where they can see what is happening—children grow into the liturgy so that it becomes a road map throughout life that guides them eventually to the gates of heaven. It doesn't seem to matter that they don't understand what the words mean at first. As they attach meaning through the questions they ask, which both parents and pastor need to answer, the words of the liturgy serve as hooks on which their life experiences can be hung and thereby attached to God. Unfortunately, some children grow up to be adults who never learn and who merely complain about things they do not understand, continuing to sit as far away from the altar as they can, missing the place where God is visibly at work. But it is not the repetitive responses in the liturgy that are at fault. The fault lies in our lack of teaching and our own unwillingness to learn what God has provided. The elderly and the dying who have grown accustomed to the liturgy during a lifetime find that what they had learned through repetition as children continues to speak meaningfully to them now, in spite of the loss of mental agility in other things that can come with aging.

THE LORD'S PRAYER

As the liturgy of the Divine Service continues, the prayers of the church reach a high point in the Preface in preparation for the celebration of Holy Communion. In the Preface we "lift up our hearts" to God and pray in unique circumstances the words of Jesus Himself in the Lord's Prayer. The Lord's Prayer is not a private prayer; it is a liturgical prayer for the community of Christ, being prayed in the plural ("Our Father"). It is important to remember that, like the Lord's Prayer, the words of the liturgy are the words of the Bible. In the Lord's Prayer, as preparation for Holy Communion, the words of Jesus take on a specific meaning for a specific response by God. Here the familiar repetition of the Lord's Prayer broadens the way to give us insight into its new meaning. Now, at this moment, in Holy Communion, God is preparing to come down from heaven to earth and feed us with His heavenly food to sustain us for more than a mere lifetime.

We pray, "Our Father who art in heaven, hallowed be Thy name, Thy kingdom come," and, as a Father, God provides for His children who call on Him. Considering what is about to happen, we call for God to come to us now as He has promised He would when His name is spoken. We are not asking for a *feeling* of God's presence, but for the actual presence of God Himself to be among us. And it is in bread and wine, the body and blood of Christ, that He comes tangibly and really. Our prayer continues, "Thy will be done on earth as it is in heaven." Here we ask God to make His *will* happen now before us in this place at the altar. For once we no longer need to ask, what is the *will* of God for me? Here it is plainly known. The *will* of God is that we receive what He comes to give. His *will* is to come to us as head of His body, the church, in these moments and commune with us on earth. He gives us what we need and what He has taught us to ask for. And so we ask God to "give us this day our daily bread." And that is exactly what God does. This day, in the bread we eat at the Lord's Supper, the bread of life, Jesus Christ is given to us. Our prayer is answered within moments of our asking.

We continue to ask, as He taught us, "Forgive us our trespasses." This is precisely why He comes down to us in this setting of the Lord's Supper. In the body and blood of Christ we are forgiven all our sins. Our prayer is about to be answered, and so we add, as Jesus taught us, "as we forgive those who trespass against us." If we have not yet forgiven (perhaps repeatedly) those we resent and hold ill feelings toward, this part in our prayer can become that time to do so. If we are still struggling with an unwillingness to forgive, this can be the time to ask for a willingness of faith to do so, even as the desperate father prayed, "I do believe; help me overcome my unbelief!" (Mark 9:24). But, if we are as yet determined not to forgive those who have sinned against us, then it is better to decline the offer of God's forgiveness for the moment, even as we decline to forgive those who have sinned against us. Such hardness of heart needs to be discussed with your pastor.

Our prayer continues, "And lead us not into temptation, but deliver us from evil." In this petition we ask God to drive out the evil at work in us that makes us unwilling to lead the new life in Christ that is given us in the heavenly food God has provided. And so we conclude, "Thine is the kingdom and the power and the glory." God governs all things with power and will destroy sin and death. God alone deserves glory and honor and praise. We have prayed the Lord's Prayer at this point in the Divine Service as a preparation for Holy Communion with God. This is the prayer that cannot be answered in private prayer in this most gracious way. Public prayer in worship prepares us for private prayer at home as private prayer at home prepares us for public prayer where God's people celebrate God's presence together "forever and ever. Amen."

Personal Devotions

There are various liturgies available for use among Christians in their private devotions at home. As with all liturgy, there is a certain formality that keeps us focused objectively on the things of God and not ourselves. Such liturgies keep us in touch with the worshiping community even as we pray in solitude. The liturgies used most by Christians down through the centuries are the liturgies written for morning, noon, early evening, or before going to bed at night. These liturgies can be found in abbreviated form in *The Lutheran Hymnal* and elsewhere. A cross, icons and religious pictures, decorative artwork, bodily gestures (sign of the cross), and positions (kneeling) help us focus our thoughts on God. Praying in the same place or time for personal devotions helps us maintain the discipline in an ongoing manner. Personally, I do well in the morning and so I have my daily personal devotions as soon as I awake. When our children were growing up, we had family devotions at the conclusion of the evening meal. Since our children have grown and left home, my wife and I continue to do this during Advent and Lent, but at other times of the liturgical year we have our shared devotions immediately before going to sleep for the night.

Responsive prayer called Suffrages can usually be found listed in the index of a liturgical hymnal. Suffrages contain an invocation, the Lord's Prayer, a creed of the Christian faith, and psalm verses that lead us to the praise of God. A short prayer called a Collect (we use the Collect from the previous Sunday) is part of the Sunday liturgy that can be used at home. A reading from the Word of God (one of the lessons from Sunday) and a concluding prayer such as Luther's Morning Prayer can be used as resources for personal or family devotions. Although the Suffrages are best used by more than one person, they can be adapted for use by one person speaking all responses to God. This liturgy used for personal devotions presents us with more than our own words and thoughts. Written prayers get us outside ourselves. Personal prayers and time for meditation can be inserted between parts of this liturgy now that they have been shaped by the Word of God. In short, liturgy gives structure and discipline to our devotions.

Liturgical prayer heals our loneliness and offers solitude both when we are alone and when we are with other people in worship. In private prayer we pour out our deepest longings for God and in public prayer we join with others who also long for God. Liturgical prayer unites us with one another as the body of Christ while at the same time allowing us to attend to our own relationship with God. Liturgical prayer is a paradox: it allows us to be alone, but not lonely, and it allows us to discover solitude even when we are not alone.

Discussion Guide

Summary

There are times in life when we must learn to be alone. Although teenage years are spent in the company of peers, they are also years when we need solitude in order to sort out things that are essential for maturity. As we begin to think about marriage in young adulthood, we may find ourselves alone in a world that makes it difficult to find a soul mate, and it can be lonely. Following the death of a spouse, loneliness is common and the solitude we have practiced throughout life becomes a time to find our companionship in God once again. As Christians pray and praise God, they find healing for their loneliness in solitude with God and in public worship with the body of Christ as the communion of saints. Healing comes in the gifts of God given in public worship. There, the solitude that comes from finding rest in God is given. Truly, as St. Augustine said, "our hearts are restless till they rest in Thee."

General Discussion

1. Describe the difference between loneliness and solitude. What is each, and how does each come about?

2. What are the strengths and weaknesses of only having personal devotions at home without the balance of public worship at church?

3. What does the formality of liturgy provide in public worship? Is *formality* a negative word in our culture? Why is "informality" preferred? What is gained or lost by either formality or informality in public worship?

4. Liturgical worship is countercultural. What does this mean?

Describe how it is countercultural. Is this a bad thing? What are the advantages of it? How might the countercultural nature of liturgy be inviting to someone in search of God?

BIBLE STUDY

Hebrews 10:23–25: How is "meeting together" in public worship an encouragement that prepares us for "the Day approaching" (v. 25)?

Hebrews 12:28: What is meant by "acceptable worship" and how does it relate to "reverence and awe" (v. 28)? Define *reverence* and *awe.* Does liturgy provide for this? How?

Hebrews 13:20–21: What elements in these verses make this a good benediction for the liturgy of public worship? Examine this "benediction" to see how the liturgy provides what the following words refer to: "God of peace," "blood of the eternal covenant," and "working in you."

Acts 2:46–47: Although the early Christians could not receive Holy Communion in the temple, they did so gathered together in their homes. They worshiped in public and at home. This witness to Word and Sacraments found "the favor of all the people" and led many to be "added to their number" (v. 47). Is it the Word and Sacraments that draws new people into the church today? Do people know what God offers in the Word and Sacraments enough to be drawn to them? Or are people looking for something other than this in joining a congregation? How can we help them discover the right thing in the liturgy of the Divine Service?

4

THE WORD OF GOD
AND THE HEALING
OF OUR DEPRESSION

Depression is common to all of us, and for some it is a major struggle. In the liturgy of the Divine Service we find healing in the Word of God as it comes to us in the words of absolution and in the Gospel message read and preached in Christ's name.

~

For years the diagnosis of clinical depression has been the most common form of mental illness known in America. Although all of us have times of "feeling depressed" to a greater or lesser degree, it is only when a person becomes immobilized by the depression and unable to function in daily living that hospitalization and medical attention are required. Volumes have been written describing both clinical and normal depression. Moments of "depression," such as we all experience at times, have been described as a common and perhaps necessary part of grief, for example, following the death of a loved one or the loss of a marriage partner in divorce. The loss of a job, investments, familiar neighborhood, or independence may cause anyone to experience a normal, temporary period of depression. Seasonal depression might recycle through a whole population of those living in parts of this country where there are long dark winters that bring life to a standstill until dispelled by the return of spring. Not infrequently, depression may occur in the lives of those who find themselves trapped in some unpleasant situation where every possible escape seems to lead nowhere. Some experience depression as a result of being trapped in a job or profession, an unhappy marriage, an unending cycle of financial difficulty, a relationship with a demanding parent, or any combination of these. The most common cause of depression for many is simply anger kept inside that builds resentment toward someone, including God.

Clinical depression has been theoretically identified as resulting from chemical deficiencies in the brain, for which antidepressants are usually prescribed. Sometimes they work, sometimes not. One antidepressant works well for one person, and another antidepressant for someone else. As frustrating and as tedious a process as it may be to find the right antidepressant that works best with the least number of side effects for any given person, such a medication may be a lifesaver for those who are suicidal. Electroshock operates on the theory that depressive thought patterns need to be rerouted by electrical stimulus. Christians ought not be afraid of making use of antidepressants, electroshock therapies, or even psychotherapy for depression, unless a particular approach to psychotherapy conflicts, in principle, with teachings of the Christian faith. It is rarely necessary, however, to pit faith against traditional medical approaches to the treatment of depression. God can work through the profession of medicine in a way that is compatible with a strong Christian faith.

There are no simple solutions to the problem of depression. As depressing as that thought may be, the truth is that we all have to learn to make the best of living with some depressing moments in life. Sometimes a depressive episode may be ended by engaging in constructive distractions, experiencing a change in weather patterns, vacationing away from stressful circumstances, or even hearing of the birth of a grandchild. When all else fails, the most hopeful prospect for the lifting of depression simply seems to be the passage of time. Depression seems to have a life span of its own, a beginning and an end, and the challenge is to survive it whether it be a matter of days, weeks, or months. For the most part, depression remains a dark mystery in the soul of man, unexplainable solely in terms of body chemistry, life situation, or personality. Spiritually, depression is simply one more part of living in a fallen world. Jesus experienced depression momentarily for us on the night before His crucifixion as He agonized over the prospect of the cross in the Garden of Gethsemane. Just as we cannot think ourselves out of depression, so Jesus as true man was helpless in His humiliation as He walked the way of the cross. He did not lift Himself out of His own depression but was lifted out of it by God through angels sent to minister to Him in His need. Our Lord rose from His knees that night in renewed strength to face death with courage and faithfulness, for us and our salvation.

It would be a misunderstanding of depression and of faith to call depression a sign of the loss of faith. Lack of faith, as with any other emotional experience, may surely accompany depression, but it is not necessarily a part of depression. Severely depressed, hospitalized patients who were able at other times to express a vibrant faith often described their depression as a *feeling* of having lost their faith. But feelings are not the same as faith. What they mean is that they "feel" abandoned by God, and yet they seldom reject God themselves. Not feeling God's presence does not mean that God is not present. I may not be aware that my wife has entered the room as I continue to be absorbed in the book I am reading, but she is there never-theless. Further, at some deeper level I do know she is there even though I am not attentive to it. The same patients who told me they "felt" they had lost their faith did not necessarily reject me as one who came in God's name to them. In fact, I often introduced myself as one who came precisely as a sign that God had not abandoned them. They needed to know God was more than their own inter-nalized feelings of either elation or dejection. They needed to know God objectively as the One outside themselves who walked with them through the "valley of the shadow" they were experiencing. My words, external to their own inner words and spoken by a pastor sent by God, brought hope, and they seemed to hold on to my words as the only tangible they had with God.

If it is implied that the depressed person, who feels he has lost his faith, is expected to recapture his own feelings of faith, he may simply despair altogether since he is being asked to do something that he simply cannot do. In fact, who of us can improve his faith, whether depressed or not, merely by trying harder? Faith is the work of the Holy Spirit within us. We ought not confuse faith and feelings. God is not a subjective feeling. He is an objective reality. For those moments when I visited a depressed patient in the hospital, I became, figuratively speaking, an incarnation of God to them—a "little Christ," as Martin Luther called the Christian. I frequently found that the depressed patient, incapable of helping herself, offered me what little trust was hers and the hope that I could help her. Faith, although sometimes accompanied by feelings, is not a feeling itself, but rather it is a relationship within which we are free to entrust, among other things, our depression to God. Most of us who experience depression will never need antidepressants or hospitalization. We will learn to live with life's depressing times through distraction, with patience, and simply through the passage of time. That is not to say, however, that we do not need help. God sends that help weekly in and through the objective liturgy of the Divine Service.

THE LITURGY GIVES VOICE TO OUR DEPRESSION

In our culture, the value we place on attending public worship seems to depend increasingly on our feelings of approval about the particulars of the service more than on the objective worth of the liturgy itself. The assumption is that if I don't feel like attending Sunday morning worship, it can't possibly do me any good to do so, as if feelings were a prerequisite for benefit. The notion that habit for its own sake is inauthentic has led us to abandon many habits that shape our lives for the better. There is no difference between taking medication in good faith that it will benefit us, simply out of habit, and attending public worship out of habit because it is beneficial to do so. Unfortunately, we have turned worship into a subjective experience that depends for its worth on us and our feelings rather than on the activity of God in that experience. Supported by this influence of our culture, many no longer worship weekly and are in danger of losing the way, the truth, and the life that is Jesus Christ. The depressed person, burdened by the weight of his depression, is unlikely to attend Sunday morning worship. As already said, it is not that the depressed person has lost faith in God, but that he has lost initiative. He cannot motivate himself to attend public worship. For this reason, the firm but gentle directiveness and assistance of a loved one in urging attendance is appropriate. The depressed person needs to attend public worship because of the objectivity of the hope it promises. It may not feel like hope, but it is objectively hopeful, for God is able to do in us what we cannot do in ourselves. Depression as a sickness of the soul and expressed subjectively as the feeling of God's absence is treated in the liturgy of the Divine Service with the medicine of the objective assurance of God's presence in Word and Sacraments.

The objectivity of the Word of God is important for the depressed person adrift in subjectivity. The depressed person may not be benefited by the insights gained in psychotherapy; in fact, she may be more depressed the more she sees of herself. Such insights about oneself are run through the filter of personal depression, which leads to a person interpreting things in the darkest way. Naming our problems in our own words does not necessarily mean we will be able to resolve them ourselves. Many of us may come to know things about ourselves better as we grow older, but that does not mean we will necessarily change our ways as a result. Human words, as insightful as they may be, do not necessarily bring benefit. Words do not help unless they carry a power from outside ourselves. In human interaction this can be seen in the power behind the words spoken by someone we love or respect in comparison with words spoken by someone whose credibility and integrity are suspect. Human words can be depressing, but the Word of God gives objective light in the darkness. This is not to say that the depressed person will receive hopeful words without running them through his depressive filter, but it is to say that the Word has power to heal nevertheless. In the interaction with God and His people at worship, the Word of God carries healing power to those who receive it in faith.

THE CONFESSION OF SINS

The liturgy, as it speaks the Word of God, gives voice to our depression and the hope of our healing. What we cannot say for ourselves because we are depressed, the liturgy helps us to speak. The deepest feelings inside us are addressed in the liturgy of the Divine Service of Word and Sacraments. Beginning with Confession, we speak aloud the spiritual reality of our depressed condition as "poor, miserable sinners." I have heard nondepressed persons say of this General Confession that they do not feel miserable at the time and wonder whether we ought to eliminate these words from the General Confession. Again, it is our cultural conditioning that convinces us that only feelings are authentic. This misunderstanding makes it difficult to grasp the objectivity of the General Confession and the liturgy itself. The words "a poor, miserable sinner" were never intended to describe our feelings of the moment; although in moments of such feelings they surely may. The words describe the reality and the fact of our condition in relationship to God, regardless of what we may feel at the moment. It is a statement of faith, not of feeling, in which we admit that in relationship to God we are, in fact, miserable sinners. It is our honest confession of sins and not our feelings that prepares us for the forgiveness that follows. Nevertheless, for the depressed worshiper these words carry both the subjective and objective content of her confession.

The liturgy follows the calendar of the church year, beginning with the Sundays of Advent and ending with the Sundays of Pentecost. The season that seems to come closest to the subject of dealing with our depression is Lent. Lent is the season of emphasis on the need for repentance in the Christian life. It is not that we do not repent throughout the year, but in Lent, as in each of the seasons of the church year, we are again reminded of the whole scope of the liturgy in addressing the deepest needs of man in relationship to God. Although in some parts of the country where winter is dark and bleak it is possible to experience depression during Lent, it is not the aim of Lent to bring about depression as somehow a penance for God's forgiveness. Lent is a season for repentance. At times when we repent due to the awareness of some devastating fault we have discovered in ourselves, we may be tempted to despair. But to give way to despair would be to neglect the main message of Lent, which is the grace of God expressed in the cross of Christ that removes despair and brings hope. Lent is not meant to be a contrived spiritual season of depression. As in the General Confession, Lent is intended to be a time of attention paid to the need in us that has been met by Christ on the cross. We dwell for six weeks on our need for God, not on our feelings of inadequacy. In so doing, we are prepared by God for the joy of Easter as the fulfillment of Christ's victory over sin in us.

THE PSALMS

The psalms in the liturgy provide the words for us to rightly approach God with our need for God's rescue. The psalm for the First Sunday in Advent invites us, "Call upon Me in the day of trouble; I will deliver you, and you will honor Me" (Psalm 50:15). The psalm as part of the Introit for the Fifth Sunday after the Epiphany also speaks hope as promise to those burdened with discouragement, "Even in darkness light dawns for the upright" (Psalm 112:4). And the psalm for the First Sunday in Lent gives us words to express our deepest despair, "Out of the depths I cry to You, O LORD; O Lord, hear my voice. . . . I wait for the LORD, my soul waits, and in His word I put my hope" (Psalm 130:1–5). The psalms continue to provide an outlet throughout the church year for our depressive moments. The psalms are among the oldest part of the liturgy, and in Christ they become the response as well as the cry for help. The Lord does not allow us to hide our feelings or our need from Him but gives us His Words to speak as the way of our healing.

THE WORD SPEAKS BACK

As the liturgy gives voice to our depression, so it also gives hope for our life. There is a light at the end of the tunnel. The depressed may not see it, but they can believe in it by faith. The liturgy, as the Word of God, leads us out of our depression and into the hope that God gives. The Old Testament Reading, the Epistle, and the Gospel assure us that, in the midst of our difficulties, disappointments, and depression, God is there to do what we cannot. God is our deliverer. If the lessons sometimes cause us grief and pain, it is to prepare us to hear the healing Word of the Gospel, the Word made flesh, Jesus, and the hope that is in Him.

In listening to the Readings each Sunday, we continually ask ourselves where in our need this Word now is at work in us. In this sense, worship requires the willingness to receive what we hear. How, in what I am going through, is God at work in me? It won't always be easy to make the connection. Hearing God speak in the Readings requires that we listen to more than words. We must listen to our own inner voice crying out for help and to the voice of God in the Reading that speaks to our cry. The importance of hearing the Word of God in times of depression, as well as any other, is that it provides a vision of what is objectively true regardless of how we feel at the moment. We need to hear the Word of hope even if we don't feel it at the moment. God's Word to the believer is always a Word of hope. This is why the depressed person needs to attend worship even when he does not feel like doing so.

There are habits of worship that need to be practiced for us to be able to receive the Word of God. One of those habits is reading the Scripture Lessons for Sunday worship before Sunday morning. Allowing time to read and think about the Readings will reawaken thought in listening to them on Sunday morning. My own habit in this is erratic, and perhaps that is why some Readings on a Sunday morning seem to pass by me without the attention they deserve. I do try to review the Introit and Collect before worship, because they are brief and they slip by too quickly in the liturgy for me to both collect my thoughts and pour out my soul in worship. It may not be possible to practice these habits all of the time, but returning to them again and again builds a repertoire of habit that prepares us to find healing in the Word of God in times of discouragement. Habits begun and practiced early in life and practiced over a lifetime tend to have their most beneficial effects on us as we grow older and no longer have the stamina to begin anew.

THE SERMON

The Word of God as sermon is where promise should be most clearly proclaimed by the pastor and recognized by the worshiper. The sermon is always, ultimately, proclamation, that is, announcement of Good News from God. The pastor may need to set the stage for us to hear God's Word as Good News by making clear our need for it, but the sermon as Word of God ought never be merely a recitation of facts or a list of moralisms to live by. It should never end on a note of anything but relief and confidence in Christ. The sermon ought not end by telling us what we must do for God, but it should end by telling us what God has done for us. The sermon is not a moralizing of how we must improve our lives, including lifting ourselves out of depression, but it must always point us outside ourselves to God, where our hope lies. Nor should the sermon give the impression that the power of our hope lies in our own faith. It lies in God's grace. If the sermon draws attention to our sins and failings, as it must do, it is only to show us the overwhelming joy of the grace and mercy that lift us above it all in Christ. This "upbeat" message is not a matter of pumping the hearer up with excitement, as if feeling excited for God is the goal. Rather, the goal is that even in the midst of persistent feelings of sadness, grief, or depression, God is always beside us through it all. Hope is not the removal of life's conflicts and depressions, but it is the gift of being able to live through them with God's help. Ultimately, it is the reality of heaven and of being with the Lord that fulfills our hope. Such fulfillment begins even now in worship, for there we are with the Lord in the best and even in the worst of times.

Discussion Guide

Summary

Faith ought never be equated with feelings. Faith is an objective relationship with God in Christ that may be expressed in feelings, but they are not the substance of it. Depression is a mood disorder that makes faith hard to express and that needs the objective attention of both the Word of God and the gift of medicine. Depression is characterized by the subjective feelings of the parishioner, whereas the liturgy of the Divine Service is characterized by the objectivity of God on our behalf. Depressed Christians need to be present in the Divine Service, which provides them with the broader vision of life that is more than the darkness that seems to surround them. There, gathered together in worship of God the Father, Son, and Holy Spirit, the community of faith stands with the depressed person when she cannot stand on her own. Surrounded by God and the family of faith, the depressed person is sustained in his depression as we all are sustained in our helplessness by God.

General Discussion

1. Without naming the person, think of someone who has experienced serious depression and, if you are willing, tell what it was like for that person.

2. Talk about normal depression. What causes you to feel "down" (weather, tiredness, etc.), and what gets you out of it?

3. How is faith something other than feelings? Can you have faith without feeling positive about life or even God at times? Is anger at God permissible as part of faith?

4. Talk about anger as causing depression. How does this work?

BIBLE STUDY

Luke 22:4–44: What signs of "depression" might Jesus have experienced as "true man" in this text? Is depression a sin? Is discouragement a sin? Is anger a sin? Could Jesus have felt any or all of these at any time you can remember in the Gospels?

Matthew 27:1–10: Judas was so depressed when he realized that he had betrayed Jesus that he committed suicide. What is the difference between the depression that Jesus may have experienced in Gethsemane and Judas's depression?

Revelation 22:1–5: In this description of the hope that awaits us as Christians, God says, "His servants will serve Him. They will see His face" (vv. 3–4). Tears, including tears of depression, are contrasted with eternity as worship. How does our weekly worship of God drive away tears temporarily now?

Galatians 6:2–5: "Carry each other's burdens. . . . For each one should carry his own load." How can we help others bear their burden of depression while recognizing that they have to bear their "own load"?

5

The Peace of the Lord and the Healing of Our Grief

In the liturgy of the Divine Service we find healing for the grief we experience at the loss of loved ones and things that have been a significant part of our lives. In commending these to God throughout the liturgy, we receive the healing peace of the Lord.

~

As I grow older, I discover an increasing need within myself to practice letting go of things and people I have enjoyed and loved in the past that have been lost to me. People die and things change. Time passes, and some friends and family with whom I once shared much have moved on to other friends or other locations or other interests. Some I have known since college days have died at a relatively young age, and their passing has left an emptiness in my life. Even those who die at a good old age are still missed and even these deaths have left their mark on me. I don't think there is anything unique in what I have experienced or felt in these losses, but they are losses, and I do grieve from time to time. Although thankful for our own ongoing lives, we also feel the pain of having been left behind to live life without these friends and family members. As painful a loss as these deaths can be, there are other losses we must also learn to live with and endure. Being a mother or a father requires us constantly to let go of our children, who need us less and less than they once did. Miles separate families, and distances are bridged in ways only partially satisfying. The loss of one's health, occasioned by chronic sickness and the limitations of aging, reminds us that even our own bodies fail us in the end. The loss of employment or retirement from the work that once gave meaning to our lives may also mean the loss of the daily affirmation we received as a result of our accomplishments and the loss of those we worked with for many years. At such times it is not easy to distinguish such losses from the perception of our loss of self-worth. All these, and other losses in life, can drain the will to live as each loss seems to contribute to the downward spiral that ends in the final loss of our own lives someday in death. It is not difficult to identify with Ecclesiastes:

> Remember your Creator in the days of your youth, before the days of trouble come and the years approach when you will say, "I find no pleasure in them" . . . before the silver cord is severed, or the golden bowl is broken; before the pitcher is shattered at the spring, or the wheel broken at the well, and the dust returns to the ground it came from, and the spirit returns to God who gave it. "Meaningless! Meaningless!" says the Teacher. "Everything is meaningless!" (Ecclesiastes 12:1–8)

Life, whatever else it brings, is a constant adjustment to our losses and the subsequent grieving that is required of us all the length of our days on earth.

In one liturgy, where the renewing strength of the Lord's Supper is not made available, the Offertory attempts to make up for it by providing us with words to express our need for hope in the face of loss. In this Offertory we sing to God, "Renew a right spirit within me. . . . Restore to me the joy of Your salvation."[17] When we have felt our losses and are ready and willing to let go of them, God gives the renewal of life and joy in Christ as a gift. Having let go of all else, we receive Christ as the fulfillment for our emptiness. Life in Christ is a constant letting go of this life and the reassurance of God's caring presence in greater and greater measure as we grow older. The Collect for the Sixth Sunday after Pentecost invites us to pray:

> O God, because You have prepared for those who love You such good things as surpass our understanding, pour into our hearts such love toward You that we, loving You above all things, may obtain Your promises, which exceed all that we can desire; through Jesus Christ, our Lord, who lives and reigns with You and the Holy Spirit, one God, now and forever. Amen.[18]

It is not as though we let go of people and things because we no longer care about them. We commend them to God's care and keeping since they are no longer ours to share as they once were. It is important, in the spiritual economy of life, to learn to "let go" so that we are increasingly prepared to receive God and need less and less things and people we have loved. This is a hard thing to understand. We do not love others less, but we grow to love God more. As Jesus said, "Anyone who loves his father or mother more than Me is not worthy of Me; anyone who loves his son or daughter more than Me is not worthy of Me; and anyone who does not take his cross and follow Me is not worthy of Me" (Matthew 10:37–38). As we ourselves finally lay at death's door, it is Christ alone who will have become our sole joy and hope. This final letting go of everyone and everything in order to receive in its place the fullness of God is tasted in the peace of the Lord we experience in the Divine Service in public worship.

If we are to live each day as a new beginning from God, we must learn to let go of yesterday. If we do not learn this, we will eventually be consumed by our own bitterness, resentment, and anger. And if it seems an impossible task to practice this "letting go," let us also remember that with God's grace at work in us all things are possible. The faith that enables us to "let go" will be rewarded by the gift of God's peace that is beyond all human understanding. Jesus reminds us, "No one who has left [let go of] home or wife or brothers or parents or children for the sake of the kingdom of God will fail to receive many times as much in this age and, in the age to come, eternal life" (Luke 18:29–30), which is to say, eternal rest . . . the peace of the Lord.

Those who do not know the Lord—the living lost of our society—propose to deal with death in their own way. Filled with fear of death, they have become stoic and resigned to it, feeling no pain. They speak of death in a way that denies its power to kill the soul as well as the body. But they protest too much, saying that death is nothing to be feared. They do not understand that death is the final curse that damns the lost. They propose, instead of reality, denial and resignation to the inevitable. Death, they say, because it is inevitable is therefore natural, and they have convinced themselves that natural is good. But all the attempts to normalize the idea of death have only obscured the dangers of doing so. It has led to taking human life without any justification other than the civil right to choose to do so. For 30 years our nation has permitted the destruction of millions of human lives through abortion. As a society we assumed that women could take the killing of a fetus in stride. The not-surprising result is that massive numbers of women have been unable to live with the grief they increasingly experience as a result of the choice to bring about the death of a child within them, something that seemed the "natural" thing to do under the circumstances of the moment. Today this normalization of death is reinforced by the Supreme Court of the land with the lame explanation that abortion is too well integrated into our culture to be reversed. The normalization of abortion continues to contribute to the normalization of death for us all.

More recently we as a nation have learned to think of death in clinical terms that again attempt to anesthetize the sting of death. The normalization of death is now being played out in the withholding of food and water from the dependent sick and the confused, inconvenient elderly as the only way, short of direct euthanasia, to bring about the death of otherwise "biologically tenacious" patients. There has been an increasing political momentum building, prompted by those who promote death as the solution to life's sufferings, that urges upon us the choice of physician-assisted suicide and euthanasia as a normal part of patient care. This atrocity of intentionally killing the suffering is already being practiced legally in the state of Oregon. As with the growing evidence of unresolved grief following abortion, so physician-assisted suicide in Oregon is already beginning to show evidence that bringing about the death of the helpless, innocent sick is not a healthy way for a society to handle the burden of suffering.

For more than a decade hospitals and nursing homes have been required by federal law to participate in the normalization of death by promoting the use of medical directives that encourage patients and families to decide how and under what circumstances their death or the death of a loved one should occur. Although it is good to think about one's death and its inevitability, there are limits to how much control over death any human being should exercise. Medical directives that promote aiming at our own death are not on the same moral level as preparing for death by choosing life until God calls us home. Self-determination, reflected in aiming at our own or another's death, is a matter of acting as if our lives were ours to do with as we please, rather than living our lives under the care of God, from whom our lives were given. Although it is possible for Christians to make use of medical directives to prevent our lives from being ended intentionally, the marketed appeal of medical directives is the opposite—that of self-determination, the way to take charge of their life, something the Christian has neither need for nor permission to do. Christians can use medical directives in a limited way; however, these directives are nevertheless a part of the culture of death that aims at the normalization of death under the self-determination of man.

In the light of abortion, physician-assisted suicide, euthanasia, and the aim of medical directives, it is not surprising that we would come to believe that death is a naturalized civil right to be exercised by the control of man. The meaning of death, however, is not ultimately determined by the mere consensus of a society. The meaning of life is provided us in the story God tells in the Divine Service on a Sunday morning. There God reveals the meaning of death as the outcome of sin and rebellion against God. In a fallen world death is the normal course of things, but God did not intend that it should be so. That death is not what God intended for us can be seen in the sting of death we still feel whenever a loved one dies or when faced with our own mortality such as at the diagnosis of a terminal illness. As a hospital chaplain, often sitting with patients as they lay dying, I almost always felt an anger rising within me after the death as I returned to my office. I wanted to cry out to God, "It ought not be this way!" Indeed, both human instinct and divine revelation point at the abnormality of death, something that "ought not be." Yet we fight against our own intuition, and we bury our anger until it breaks out unexpectedly emotionally or in physical illness. It was not until I turned to God in prayer, following each death, that I was able to let go and let death itself die in Christ. In Christ's victorious death we find the peace of the Lord that enables us to continue the life to which God has called us. The words of the liturgy "Peace be with you," spoken each Lord's Day, become increasingly important as the number of losses increases in life. In the liturgy of the Divine Service God gently pries loose our desperate grasp on those we have loved and lost and restores to us the life that is eternal in Himself.

One Offertory of the Divine Service, taken from Psalm 116, especially provides us opportunity to express our grief and find healing. The psalmist is trying to come to terms with his losses. The message of grief and its healing is missed if this is ignored. The context of the Offertory is given at the beginning of the psalm. Verse 3 defines the theme—"The cords of death entangled me, the anguish of the grave came upon me; I was overcome by trouble and sorrow." In response to the psalmist's experience of loss through the death of loved ones, he turns to God in worship. "Then I called on the name of the LORD." Throughout the psalm the psalmist can be seen moving from grief to healing, writing, "Precious in the sight of the LORD is the death of His saints" (v. 15). The middle section of this psalm provides us with the words chosen for the Offertory. What might have escaped us, had we not known the context, are words provided for us by God, expressing our healing. We sing Psalm 116 beginning with verse 12:

> What shall I render to the Lord for all His benefits to me? I will offer the sacrifice of thanksgiving and will call on the name of the Lord. I will take the cup of salvation and will call on the name of the Lord. I will pay my vows to the Lord now in the presence of all His people, in the courts of the Lord's house, in the midst of you, O Jerusalem.[19]

We are now ready to come before the altar with angels and archangels and all the company of heaven, "to the church of the firstborn, whose names are written in heaven . . . to the spirits of righteous men made perfect"

(Hebrews 12:23). Here, we stand with those who have died in faith and who were once lost to us. I have heard people say that they cannot attend public worship because they become too emotionally upset following the recent loss of a loved one, but there is nothing wrong with quiet tears in worship. Even greater than the tears of grief and loss expressed in public worship are the tears of joy that come in rediscovering loved ones at worship with us among the host of heaven.

The words of the Preface, sung or spoken by the pastor, end with the proclamation that the heavens are now opening before us. The pastor concludes, "Therefore with angels and archangels and with all the company of heaven we laud and magnify Your glorious name, evermore praising you and saying."[20] And the congregation in heaven and the congregation on earth join together in singing, "Holy, holy, holy Lord, God of power and might: Heaven and earth are full of Your glory. Hosanna. Hosanna. Hosanna in the highest. Blessed is He who comes in the name of the Lord. Hosanna in the highest."[21]

At this point in the Divine Service the curtain separating this life from the next is drawn back and we sing with those who have gone before us the glory of Christ's victory over sin and death. Here, in the Divine Service, as nowhere else on earth, we are together as one, saints above and saints on earth. Here, more than anywhere else in this life, we are near to those who have died in Christ. No memories or private devotions can rival the reality that all the community of heaven worships with us when we worship together in the Divine Service on a Sunday morning. What better place to find healing and reunion with loved ones than in the gathering of God's people before the altar?

With the coming of God down from heaven in His body and blood in Holy Communion we have before us that moment for which the liturgy has been preparing us from the beginning. In this moment there is no room for anything but God so that we both consume and are consumed by Him. This is the greatest moment of our loss and our gain. As we lose ourselves in Christ, we regain eternal life. Here, in the celebration of the Lord's Supper, we experience the healing that begins with letting go of everything else in this life. For a moment we have no grief, no anger or bitterness, no sadness or distress, no losses— only joy and gain. It is enough to set us on the path of daily living as hope revives each Sunday morning in experiencing heaven on earth in the Divine Service, where God Himself serves us for the healing of the nations.

When my father died some years ago, I grieved for him. I missed being able to share things with him and talk of things I discovered or did that he would have enjoyed. Although I occasionally continue to have such moments of remembrance of things we shared, what I have enjoyed more than anything in remembering him is the way he sang in church on a Sunday morning. Dad did not have a trained voice, nor was it a loud voice, but it was loud enough to become part of the congregation's joy. I can't remember him singing around the house, but his voice was true and constant in singing both liturgy and hymns in church. As he grew older, his voice became thinner and strained as he tried to reach the notes, but he sang with his heart as well as his voice. Now, in my 60s, I sing with similar abandon, modeling myself after one of the saints that sat beside me in the pew for a lifetime. Of special significance is the moment when Dad and I continue to sing side by side in the Divine Service as heaven and earth are joined in the body of Christ. It is no mere sentimental occasion, but rather a hearty one, that puts both Dad and me at the foot of God's throne as brothers in Christ. My grief following his death is healed, and my occasional tears are tears of joy for what we both continue to share, he in heaven and I on earth. There will always be a bittersweet ambivalence the Christian feels as he waits for the day when he too will join the saints in heaven as part of the eternal worship of God that we taste in part on a Sunday morning in the Divine Service on earth. Paul himself expressed it saying, "I desire to depart and be with Christ, which is better by far; but it is more necessary for you that I remain in the body" (Philippians 1:23–24). Until that day when all tears are wiped away, we are given the gift of the Divine Service, where saints in this life and the next join together in the praise of God—Father, Son, and Holy Spirit.

Discussion Guide

Summary

Death is the curse we have brought on ourselves through our sin as a people. There is no easy way to grieve and no human way to remove the pain that reminds us that we, too, will die someday. But in spite of the depressing nature of these realities, there is a greater reality that overcomes all hopelessness. Jesus' death is the heart and substance of the Christian faith, because in His death our death has become a mere sleep. As He rose, we, too, will rise. The Divine Service is the one place on earth where heaven and earth meet so that we who live and they who live eternally are joined temporarily in the worship of God even as we will be in a greater measure permanently in heaven. In the Divine Service God heals our grief and gives us a taste of the peace of God that will be ours forever.

General Discussion

1. Talk about the kinds of things people feel when they grieve. What kinds of things interfere with getting over grief?

2. What do you think happens to people's grief when they do not express it and keep it inside? How does "talking" help someone adjust to a loss (death or something else)?

3. Do you feel closer to loved ones who have died when you worship in church? What, in the liturgy, is particularly meaningful to you when you think of a loved one who has died?

4. Review the concluding words of the Preface. Have you ever realized that this is the beginning of heaven on earth that comes to us in the bridge of Christ's body and blood? How does this reality offer healing for our grief?

BIBLE STUDY

Revelation 4:1–11 describes the setting of heaven as an eternal worship service. When you worship God in the Divine Service, are there ever moments when you wish it would not end? What is it in human nature that resists the worship of God?

Revelation 19:1–10 describes worship in heaven as a wedding feast. How is the celebration of Holy Communion in the Divine Service "a foretaste of the feast to come"?

Hebrews 12:1–2 says that the crowd of witnesses who have lived and died before us encourage us to continue to be faithful to the end. How might we "throw off everything that hinders" in the Divine Service, as Hebrews 12:1 says?

Hebrews 4:14–16: How does Jesus facing trials and temptations help us in dealing with our grief before God in public worship?

6

THE PRAYERS OF THE CHURCH AND THE HEALING OF OUR SICKNESS

Jesus healed the sick of their physical and mental illnesses, and the church has always followed in the steps of our Lord by praying for the healing of those in the congregation and community. The liturgy of the Divine Service does this in the Prayer of the Church.

~

We pray in the Sunday morning liturgy for the healing of those sick and hospitalized members of our congregation and their families and friends because Jesus' ministry took the form of physical as well as spiritual healing. Jesus' healing ministry demonstrated the close relationship between forgiveness and healing, a flowing of the spiritual into the physical and the physical into the spiritual. This is difficult for us to understand in our times and in our particular culture. We are living at a time in our thinking when the spiritual has become separated from the material. It is hard for us to understand ages past that seemed to make no distinction between the two. Some call those past ages superstitious. Of course, superstition can exist in any age, but not all belief in the connection between the spiritual and the material world is superstitious. The skeptic's argument today is that since all we can see is the material world, that's all there must be to life. It is assumed that all illness is simply the result of bodily malfunctions that, in theory, can be corrected. This is especially the view of many working in the area of science and research. Most recently we have come to believe that virtually all illness can be explained as malfunctioning genes. Genes, researchers tell us, hold the key to unlocking the mystery of illness once and for all. But this purely materialist view of illness does not allow for questions about why some genes are "turned on" in some people, causing illness, while those same genes are not turned on in others. No doubt scientists will be able to explain such inconsistencies, in part, in terms of environmental differences. Although these materialistic explanations may be true, they are not the whole story of illness, since such a narrow view of illness lacks the spiritual key to the meaning of illness as the result of living in a "fallen world." Because this reality is not accepted by many researchers, scientists and others continue to grasp life from the hands of God to remake it in the image of man.

Christians are often charged with interfering in the progress of genetic research by raising ethical questions and suggesting there ought to be limits to what we do to, and with, human lives made in the image of God. At the same time, as science pursues a materialistic approach to illness, the way we view the distinction between spiritual and material understanding of illness in our culture is also changing in the public eye. In recent history it has taken us decades to begin to recognize again the relationship of the tangible to the intangible, the mind to the body, the spiritual to the physical. We have begun to use the word *holistic* to describe this more inclusive approach to illness that recognizes the importance of the spiritual care of the sick. Additionally, there are forms of alternative medicine continually being proposed to address the need for care that doesn't fit under the protocol of scientific medicine. It remains to be seen whether all of these holistic alternatives are beneficial or are, in some cases, merely a rebellion against the narrowness of scientific medicine. We have had our eyes opened once again to the realization that there is more to life than meets the eye. Christians have before them an opportunity to direct those suffering illness to Jesus Christ, the healer of the nations, in whom we find life forevermore.

Christians can appreciate the wholeness of the spiritual and the physical as two sides of the same coin that enriches our lives. That richness is evident in the liturgy of the Divine Service and the Prayer of the Church, where Christians place before God their hope of wholeness in Jesus Christ. The prayers for healing in our liturgical setting of the Divine Service come after we have been cleansed of sin and made ready to stand before God in order to make our requests of God on behalf of the sick and hospitalized. When after the Confession and Absolution we sing the Kyrie, "Lord, have mercy; Christ, have mercy; Lord, have mercy,"[22] we are not asking for God's mercy because of our sins. They have been forgiven. We are asking for God's mercy in hearing and answering our prayers, among them our prayers for healing. Our prayers in public worship always begin with praise, in particular the Hymn of Praise, following the Kyrie. There is a choice offered to us in the liturgy between two Hymns of Praise. They each contain the actual words of God delivered to us by angels as recorded in Luke 2:14, the Gloria in Excelsis, and in Revelation 5:9–13 and 19:4–9, This Is the Feast. Our sung praises are followed by God's response to our prayers, beginning with the Lessons and then the Sermon. In God's Word, preached as Law and Gospel, God prepares us to make our requests of Him in a spirit of humility because of our sinful nature and in the spirit of confidence because of God's mercy and grace.

All healing comes from God and by God's grace, whether given to believer or nonbeliever. Healing comes through the gifts God gives in medical treatment, and it comes in the Word spoken in public worship. I recently attended a service of worship at a congregation while on vacation far from my home in which I brought with me a brokenness in myself that had been in need of healing for many weeks. It was in the Sermon that God's Word spoke healing to me. The text was Luke 10:25–37, the story of the Good Samaritan. This text could easily have been used as Law in a moralizing way that tells us how we ought to care for others, but the pastor resisted this approach and proclaimed the text as Gospel, showing us that the broken and battered man on his way to Jericho was each of us. The Good Samaritan who cares for us and provides our healing is Jesus. As the Good Samaritan, Jesus pours out the wine of His blood on our wounds, wraps them gently, and carries us to the inn of His keeping, where we find healing. Because I came to public worship that Sunday morning battered and bruised with disappointment and frustration, and because the pastor preached the text as a Gospel text, I experienced healing that rid me of my own physical, mental, and spiritual illness. This healing freed me to think of the needs of others without a moralizing of the text. My prayers for healing had begun before the service in the pew as I meditated even amid the many distractions of conversations around me. My prayers found their response in the Gospel, where healing is left to God, and not in trying harder to change myself. Although this particular service of worship offered only the Word and did not offer the Sacrament of the Altar, God proclaimed healing in the Word, which affected both soul and body as the physical symptoms of my distress disappeared and peace and joy returned to my life.

There is no clear line drawn between the spiritual and the physical in the Gospel Jesus proclaims. Healing of both body and soul begins here and is brought to completion in eternity, where we will see Him and worship Him face-to-face. Our weekly worship in the liturgy anticipates this face-to-face encounter with God by giving us a glimpse of God in the Divine Service of Holy Communion. This weekly worship prepares Christians for eternity, where they will see His face and find healing forevermore:

> Then the angel showed me the river of the water of life, as clear as crystal, flowing from the throne of God and of the Lamb down the middle of the great street of the city. On each side of the river stood the tree of life,

bearing twelve crops of fruit, yielding its fruit every month. And the leaves of the tree are for the healing of the nations. No longer will there be any curse. The throne of God and of the Lamb will be in the city, and His servants will serve Him. They will see His face, and His name will be on their foreheads. . . . And they will reign for ever and ever. (Revelation 22:1–5)

Jesus' critics were angry that He performed His ministry of forgiving sins and healing diseased bodies because by it, they said, He was claiming to be the God of all creation. We who worship Him believe He is exactly that, and so we come to Him with our prayers for healing of both body and soul.

This connection between spirituality and the physical world is acceptable to many people in our culture, whether they are "religious" or not. Spirituality has come to mean any form of meditation or thought that detaches the mind from the troubles of the day. As unfortunately pagan in nature as such spirituality is, it leaves the way open for us as Christians to introduce a real spirituality that has substance and truth. As a hospital chaplain I seldom met a physician who did not respect the vocation I represented as "physician of the soul," because most physicians recognized that healing belongs ultimately to the realm of mystery and not to science. Although researchers are able to discover the mechanisms of healing and may increasingly learn to manipulate them, those who care for patients at the bedside, both doctors and nurses, know that illness is more than germs and genes. Some know the mystery of illness and the healing that links the spiritual and the physical into one and the same experience in the cross of Christ.

Matthew Harrison reminds us of the importance of

seeing healing in a holy perspective under the cross of Christ:

> If Christ today dwells in His church via His Gospel preached and Sacraments administered, can we deny that there is healing going on in the church today? Who of us would deny it? Who of us has not seen personally a remarkable turn of medical events in an individual for whom we prayed, to whom we [pastors] administered the Sacrament? Yet, we must admit, that in this mean time, all the glory of Christ lies veiled under the cross. Lazarus was raised, but he soon died a second death. None of us can escape the portal through which we must leave this life. So there's no point in putting "healing" or "wholeness" at the center of our theology. That would displace Christ and His cross. "Wholeness" remains secondary; always contingent upon the cross as Christ wills it for His purposes in this life, and fully only in the next.[23]

What Harrison is saying is that, although we pray rightly when we ask for the healing of the sick and dying, our faith does not rest on whether God answers our prayers such as we wish them to be answered. Our faith rests, rather, on Jesus Christ and His working through our illnesses for His purposes. It is important that we do not call upon God conditionally, putting God to the test and saying in effect, "I will ask God to heal my wife (husband, child, parent) of this illness, but if He doesn't, I will have nothing more to do with Him." Few of us would actually say this aloud, but there is a grumbling voice deep within each of us that wearies from years of prayers for healing that seem to go unanswered. We must remember Abraham, who waited a lifetime for God's promise of a son to be fulfilled only to have God ask Abraham to offer that son as a sacrifice. What possible reason could God have had for placing such a burden on Abraham? Whatever it meant to Abraham, it is surely clear now that the sacrifice demanded of Abraham was substituted in God's sacrifice of His only begotten Son for us all.

Our prayers for the healing of disease and injury may seem to go unanswered, but we are always called to love God, not for what we can get out of Him, but for God's own sake even when the silence is deafening. "All things God works for the good of those who love Him" (Romans 8:28), but the good often remains veiled under the cross of Christ even as it is also veiled under the cross we bear in His name. Illness is a mystery not only for the researcher and physician, but also for the world as it groans in exile, waiting for the healing of the nations.

Jesus is the bridge between the spiritual and the physical world. When God took on human form as a child born in Bethlehem, He engaged the kingdom of this physical world for reconciliation with the kingdom of God. Jesus' birth is the beginning of God's healing of the whole creation that groans in waiting for its adoption by God. As Jesus came to heal, so He sent His disciples out to anoint the sick with oil and the laying on of hands. "Calling the Twelve to Him, He sent them out two by two and gave them authority over evil spirits. . . . They drove out many demons and anointed many sick people with oil and healed them" (Mark 6:7–13).

Some congregations continue this ministry, scheduling public liturgies throughout the year for the healing of the sick and for those with special needs. One Lutheran liturgy for use as public worship includes the laying on of hands and the anointing of the sick. Martin Luther encouraged this rite of healing for the sick. The Roman Catholic Church, in the 1970s, followed Luther's recommendations for reforming the church's teaching on "Last Rites" to become a rite of "The Anointing of the Sick." The rite of anointing is to be offered at the beginning of an illness rather than at the end of life as had been the case with Last Rites. The Lutheran rite of anointing and laying on of hands emphasizes the grace of God, rather than the faith of the one seeking healing. This distinguishes it from "faith healing" as practiced by others. The Lutheran rite is liturgical, using the Apostles' Creed, the Readings for the week, the Prayer of the Day, a Sermon, Hymns, Prayers, and Benediction. At one point in the service the rubrics (instructions) say:

> Those who wish to receive laying on of hands (and anointing) come to the altar and, if conditions permit, kneel. The minister lays both hands on each person's head in silence, after which he may dip a thumb in the oil and make the sign of the cross on the person's forehead, saying, "O God, the giver of health and salvation; As the apostles of our Lord Jesus Christ, at His command, anointed many that were sick and healed them, send now Your Holy Spirit, that *name*, anointed with this oil, may in repentance and faith be made whole; through the same Jesus Christ our Lord."[24]

There is also a nonpublic service for laying on of hands and anointing of the sick for individuals. This, too, is a liturgical rite in that it places emphasis on the action of God rather than the responses of man. It includes a private confession of sins followed by absolution, the Lessons, and the laying on of hands with optional anointing with oil. When the sick are anointed "in the name of the Father and of the Son and of the Holy Spirit," a brief prayer follows and then the Benediction. It is meant for use at the bedside, at home, or in a hospital.

There are also other liturgies that serve to heal, such as the liturgy of individual Confession and Absolution and celebration of Holy Communion. As with the corporate service of healing, forgiveness of sins and the prayer for physical healing go hand in hand, again recognizing that the spiritual and the physical are inextricably entwined. In all, these liturgies remind us that Jesus' healing accompanied His preaching because the Word of God is a healing and reconciling Word. God is a gracious God, who willingly suffered and died for us so that our present suffering would be comforted by His victory on the cross. Therefore, we pray for one another that we might be healed forevermore.

Discussion Guide

Summary

We usually think of the hospital as the place we go to when physically sick or injured and the church as the place we go to for spiritual healing and care. But the fact that we pray for the sick in public worship says something more about the connection between physical illness and spiritual well-being. We acknowledge that physical illness is a symptom of the underlying condition of this fallen world called sin. Our own sinful nature needs the attention of God if it is to find healing and we are to live. A visit from the pastor when we become hospitalized is a sign of this connection, as is our weekly worship when we pray for the sick. In a world that increasingly treats illness merely as a malfunctioning of genes, Christians need to remember that the mystery of illness is deeper than the mental or physical. We need the cure that no medicine can give: the Healer, Jesus Christ!

General Discussion

1. What do you think causes illness? What role does stress play in causing illness? Is stress itself a sign of spiritual need?

2. What does it mean when we pray for the healing of the sick by name in the liturgy? How does our praying for them help us as well as them?

3. What do you think of the idea of periodically scheduling a liturgy for the healing of the sick? of anointing? of the laying on of hands for healing?

4. Have you been prayed for in public worship? What did it mean to you? Do you request the prayers of the church when you or a family member is seriously ill? If not, why not?

BIBLE STUDY

Luke 11:1–13 urges us to pray for healing. What do you make of the connection in verse 13 between healing and the Holy Spirit? How does the work of the Holy Spirit address the underlying condition of sickness in the soul?

Matthew 9:1–8: What point does the healing of this man's physical disability make in relationship to the Gospel? Is physical healing an end in itself or a means to an end or both? Why?

Hebrews 10:19–25 speaks of the connection between worship and acts of "love and good works" such as caring for the sick. According to this passage, what is the connection between worship and good works (caring for the sick)?

Revelation 22:1–5: Believers in Christ already share in the eternal life described here. Where do we experience the "water of life" and the "healing of the nations" and "see His face" now in our weekly worship in the liturgy of the Divine Service?

7

THE CREED
AND THE HEALING
OF OUR INTELLECT

We are all in need of healing in the way we learn to think about this life. We need a healing of the intellect that God provides in the liturgy of the Divine Service in the content of the Creed. Here, our subjective ways of thinking about life are given objectivity as God's thoughts become our thoughts.

~

L iturgical worship makes use of the three historic ecumenical creeds of the Christian church known as the Apostles' Creed, the Nicene Creed, and the Athanasian Creed. The Athanasian Creed, due in part to its length as well as its content, is generally reserved for use on the Feast of the Holy Trinity. The Apostles' Creed is generally used in liturgies where Holy Communion is not celebrated. The Nicene Creed is used most frequently in the liturgy of the Divine Service where Holy Communion is celebrated. All three historic creeds serve the need for our intellectual healing because they objectify the Gospel message in the Christian's way of thinking about God and life, a contrast with the myopia of any contemporary reading of the meaning of life in our time. Human intellect without the Gospel is continually in the process of attempting to rewrite the story God tells about the meaning of life.

Gene Edward Veith, in a chapter from *Postmodern Times* titled "Constructing and Deconstructing the Truth," describes the way we have been taught to think in our times: "Deconstructionists cultivate what they call 'subversive readings.' Language does not reveal meaning [which would imply that there is an objective, transcendent realm of truth]; rather, language constructs meaning. ... The meaning-making process is taken apart. The text is thereby 'deconstructed.'"[25]

This contemporary way of thinking was expressed more commonly by one of my students when she said, "My sister-in-law made use of donor sperm to become pregnant, and I like my sister-in-law, so I don't see anything wrong with it." As Veith says, how we think about what is right and wrong in postmodern times is not a matter of what is objectively right or wrong, but of what we like or don't like. Spiritual beliefs are expressed by the postmodern skeptic with words such as, "I don't like the idea of hell, therefore I don't believe in hell." In contemporary thought the truth about reality is not what we discover to be true, but what we like and therefore make true for ourselves. The thinking of many in our culture has become almost entirely subjective rather than objective.

The Word of God seems to have little authority to shape the way we think and therefore live in this culture because it claims to speak objectively for all people of all times. Our contemporary way of thinking does not *like* what it hears from God. I must admit that as much as I recognize this way of thinking is in need of healing, the same thinking has rooted itself deep in my own mind as well. I, too, find, for example, that when I am in a hurry, I tend not to come to a complete stop at a stop sign and not to obey the speed limit because I do what I *like* to do rather than what I *should* do. As a willing participant in my own sinful nature, it is only when I feel threatened by the unpleasant possibilities of receiving a citation from the police that I reluctantly alter my subjective likes and dislikes for that moment. And yet, as someone continually transformed by the Gospel, I confess in the Creed each week that my life is also being given over to Christ, who lives in me so that I more often willingly obey even the laws of the road for the good of all. Each Christian is a strange mixture of sinner and saint at the same time. We do not easily recognize the need for healing of the intellect, and therefore our thinking, since it requires of us that we admit our thinking may be sick. Indeed, it is impossible for the sick mind to recognize its own sickness, and we need an external "second opinion" from God to see it.

It is easier to pray for physical healing of physical illness than it is to pray for healing of one's own intellect. The only healing of our mind's thinking that seems somewhat easier to pray for is that ambivalence in thinking that causes us emotional pain, as in grief, fear, panic, or depression. It is much harder for us to think that our well-ordered, rational thinking may also be in need of healing. We easily give in to our sinful human nature that likes to think for itself. Yet every generation from Adam to the present has needed healing at the core of its thinking. Why? Because our intellect is in conflict with God. When Adam and Eve were tempted to think for themselves rather than receive the truth of God, they suffered and began to die of it. The tempter deconstructed the Word of God, saying, "You will not die." Our first parents liked that revision of God's words. Although God's Word has always been challenged by humankind, the uniqueness of the challenge today lies in the difficulty we have of even believing there is any such thing as objective truth. We think we need to think on our own because there is nothing else out there. We are in need of a healing of the intellect in this matter!

Without healing of the intellect, we will assume all thinking about reality is subjective. This means we will think all experiences in life mean only what we think they mean. A parallel to this can be seen in art appreciation today. It is difficult to find an artist who paints or sculpts as a way of conveying truth. The artist prefers to invite us to read into the artwork whatever meaning is our own. In contrast, the healed intellect will be able to distinguish one's own thoughts from the objective reality provided by God. The extreme of the one who believes all reality is subjective is the person who, having had a mental breakdown, thinks he can fly like Superman if he jumps off a tall building. It is not uncommon to find a patient in the psychiatric unit of any given hospital who thinks he is Jesus Christ. We clearly recognize these people as having experienced a break with reality in their thinking—they have lost objectivity—but we are reluctant to identify the same tendency in ourselves.

Strangely, there are those whose claim to objectivity is also a result of a breakdown of intellect. For example, there are those zealous for objectivity who believe whatever they do is the objective, determined will of God and make little distinction between their own thoughts and the thoughts of God. These well-meaning but dangerous zealots, found in every religion, are in need of healing because they have subjectively confused their own thinking with what they believe to be the objective thoughts of God Himself. The thinking of these people is usually characterized by actions that lack empathy for others. They are unreasonable and unfair in their demands on others. And they are ultimately destructive and hostile toward human lives. This, too, is clearly a distortion of objectivity that we recognize as something other than the objective Word of God, received and delivered to us by prophets and apostles and recorded as the written Word of God, the Bible. No man can hope to grasp the whole of God so that whatever he says can always claim to be the Word from God to us. Healing of the intellect by means of the Gospel means that we will be able to make the distinction between our own thoughts and the thoughts of God. This distinction may become fuzzy to any of us at times, but in the healing that comes through the Gospel we will ultimately be kept truthful through the working of the Holy Spirit as Christ lives in us.

THE NICENE CREED

The Nicene Creed, confessed in the liturgy of the Divine Service, keeps our intellect and objectivity healthy.

In it we hear not only the truth about God, but also the truth about ourselves and this life. Each of the three articles or parts of the Creed speaks to us in our time as it has to every generation.

Our confession of faith begins as follows:

> I believe in one God, the Father Almighty, maker of heaven and earth and of all things visible and invisible.

The oneness of God is clarified in our thinking as we speak God's name as Father, Son, and Holy Spirit. This contrasts with the thinking of many today who like to believe all religions worship the same God. Indeed, there are some who choose to create their own "Higher Power"—something that may be as inanimate as a tree, the wind, or a cherished idea. The influence of Eastern religions is appealing to some because they can choose their deity according to their likes and dislikes, in contrast with traditional Western Christian beliefs. These subjective beliefs in God are rejected by those who confess in the Creed that God comes to us not on our terms, but on His and has revealed Himself as "the Father Almighty, maker of heaven and earth."

In our brave new world of reproductive technologies and genetic manipulations, laboratory-grown children and human cloning incite our curiosity and consume our imagination. How exciting to take human life into our own hands and be the "maker of heaven and earth and of all things visible and invisible," remaking the world in our own image so that our subjectivity becomes the new religion! In Huxley's futuristic classic,[26] this brave new world has no room for the designations "mother and father" since all children are conceived and bred in the laboratory where their conditioning can be shaped to fit the liking of others. Our confession of God as Father Almighty stands over and against this thinking and proclaims to the world that we have only one God and Father of us all whose creative powers are continued in the procreation of children through husband and wife in the one-flesh union of marriage. Our thinking otherwise is in need of healing. Human subjectivity that likes it otherwise is what brought down Adam and Eve and made this a fallen world where it has become common to want to be our own god and deny the objective reality of the only God there is or could ever be, the Father Almighty.

The Nicene Creed continues:

> And in one Lord Jesus Christ, the only-begotten Son of God, begotten of His Father before all worlds, God of God, Light of Light, very God of very God, begotten, not made, being of one substance with the Father, by whom all things were made; who for us men and for our salvation came down from heaven and was incarnate by the Holy Spirit of the virgin Mary and was made man; and was crucified also for us under Pontius Pilate. He suffered and was buried. And the third day He rose again according to the Scriptures and ascended into heaven and sits at the right hand of the Father. And He will come again with glory to judge both the living and the dead, whose kingdom will have no end.

God reveals Himself as both unity and diversity; He is one God—Father, Son, and Holy Spirit. This article of the Creed speaks of God the Son as being one with the Father, "God of God, . . . begotten, not made, being of one substance with the Father." The distinction between being "begotten" and being "made" is clarified as meaning that the Son of God is "one substance with the Father." This clarification is important for our thinking about God and ourselves particularly at this time in history.

It is important that we know that the Father and the Son are of the same substance as a way of saying that Jesus is nothing less than God, even though He became incarnate as man. It was clear to Jesus' contemporaries that He claimed to be God in the flesh. His critics rejected His claim, but they knew what it was He claimed for Himself. Whether people of our own time are clear about who Jesus Christ claims to be will depend, as it always has, on whether there is faith to receive this truth. Of importance for Christians today who look to God to understand their own lives is the concept of being "begotten, not made" as it applies to children "made" in the laboratory as compared to children "begotten" of their parents in the act of procreation. This distinction is particularly important in the "making" of children by means of donor sperm or egg or the "making" of a child for the woman who chooses not to marry or the "making" of children through human cloning. The ongoing debate about what to do with leftover human embryos in the lab underscores the human waste mentality that treats human life as disposable according to the will of man. If the Son is begotten of the Father, it is also the message of the Christian faith that children were meant to be of the same substance as their parents and not the created substance of researchers, scientists, and others whose thinking has become unhealthy and in need of healing.

The Son of God is confessed in that "He suffered and was buried. And the third day He rose again according to the Scriptures." Christians know the significance of the death and resurrection of Jesus for our reconciliation with God, but it is the authority of this claim that is in question in our subjective age. I recall a man, suspicious of the Christian claim, who challenged the Nicene Creed, saying, "After all, pastor, no one really knows if Jesus was God. Even the Creed throws doubt on it by saying it is only 'according to the Scriptures.' Who really knows?" He had taken this affirmation of faith as a qualification expressing the doubt even of believers. He assumed all we had to go on was "according to the Scriptures," and they might not be accurate. But the confession of the Creed is an affirmation, not a qualification of our faith. "According to the Scriptures" means in accord (agreement) with Old Testament Scripture, now fulfilled in Christ. The subjectivism that calls into question every claim of truth is in need of healing by the objective witness of the Creed, which Christians have confessed for millennia.

The Creed concludes:

> And I believe in the Holy Spirit, the Lord and giver of life, who proceeds from the Father and the Son, who with the Father and the Son together is worshiped and glorified, who spoke by the prophets. And I believe in one holy Christian and apostolic Church, I acknowledge one Baptism for the remission of sins, and I look for the resurrection of the dead and the life of the world to come. Amen.

With His resurrection and return to the Father Almighty, Jesus sent the Holy Spirit to make effective the work of the Gospel in us as the "one holy Christian and apostolic Church." We are the body of Christ on earth to continue His ministry to the world. The Holy Spirit prepares us for this ministry through the liturgy of the Divine Service, in Word and Sacraments, through "Baptism for the remission of sins" even as we "look for the resurrection of the dead and the life of the world to come." This is our mission and our purpose in life. Whatever our vocation, the underlying ministry of God through us to others is the vocation of Christ living out His life in us in this world.

This stands in contrast to a world that has lost its way, intellectually floundering in search of a reason to live and not die. Preoccupied with immortality through the cure of disease and the hope of restoring life to the dead, our world sees little more to life than living as an end in itself. Our world lacks a future hope of fulfillment. It is a world in which lost souls try to make the best of this life because it appears that is all there is left to do. Energies in research are centered on physical well-being while souls die for lack of meaning to life. Relief of suffering and pain becomes the highest priority for medicine today, but to what end? There is hope for little more than to survive and avoid the void that awaits lost humankind in death. Such thinking of these things is in need of healing!

The health of our hope is confessed each week in the words of the Nicene Creed. There we affirm with confidence the promises of God that this life is not all there is to life. There we are given the bill of health that assures us of a future with God the Father Almighty; His only-begotten Son, Jesus Christ; and the Holy Spirit, the Lord and giver of life. Our hope of heaven is not merely that we gain "more life," but that we gain the eternal life Himself, Jesus Christ. As the way, the truth, and the life, He is our fulfillment in this life and the next. This good news about God is good news about us and our mission, purpose, and vocation. The Creed is not only about God. It is about us and our life with God in this world and the next. This truth is no subjective opinion. It is the objective fact of faith that we confess loud enough for each of us to hear from one another in worship as we prepare to go out into our world with the Gospel of peace.

Discussion Guide

Summary

Luther called human reason "a whore"—but only in reaction to those who said that we can intellectually achieve our own salvation. Sometimes Christians attack intellect as the enemy, but Jesus calls us to serve Him with our mind as well as the body. We live in times that highlight emotion, not intellect. Education is failing in this culture because we devalue intellect and truth in favor of experience and freedom of action. God heals intellect and gives us a reasonable approach to problem solving that lifts us above our own needs and wants. In the Creed we proclaim intelligibly the content of our faith as a reminder that the content of our faith is not what we would "like" it to be, but what God has made it to be. In a culture that believes there is no transcendent truth, this confession of faith is both offensive and necessary to the world's salvation.

General Discussion

1. How much do people's "likes" determine what they believe? Do you only believe what you like? Is it necessary to like everything the Christian faith is about? For example, do you like it that God will come "to judge both the living and the dead"?

2. One symptom of the sickness of our way of thinking (intellect) today is the way many define morality in subjective terms that allow them to do whatever they want to do. How do you see some of this same attitude in your own life? What is it about our subjective way of life that is in need of healing?

3. Luther, as well as St. Paul, did not believe that a person could come to faith by reason, but Luther used reason to explain the faith in his catechism. What is the relationship between faith and reason?

4. The three creeds of the Christian faith keep the content of the faith objective. They are a summary of what the Bible says. Why do we speak the Nicene Creed in public worship? What does it do for us as a congregation? as an individual?

BIBLE STUDY

1 Corinthians 1:18–30: Why did God want to destroy "the wisdom [intellect] of the wise" (v. 19)? Who are these wise? Is it wrong to be wise? What is the problem here?

What does it mean that Christ is a "stumbling block" to the wise (v. 23)? Do we have to give up our thinking when we become a Christian and believe "blindly"? Are Christians against intel- lect?

What is the difference between being a "fool for Christ" and just being a "fool"? In verse 30 we are told Jesus Christ is the One who became for us "wisdom from God." How does Christ as our Wisdom enable us to intellectually understand the world around us better?

2 Timothy 2:14–19: Paul warns us not to argue (reason) con- tentiously with others about the Christian faith. He tells each of us to present (proclaim) the message as one who rightly han- dles the "word of truth" (v. 15). What is the difference between contentiously "disputing about words" and "rightly handling the word of truth"?

CONCLUSION

For sinful people living in a fallen world, worshiping God rightly is a learned activity taught by God, not an activity we are expected to perfect on our own. From the beginning of the world it has been the fallenness of human nature that has led to the worship of idols rather than the worship of the one true God. It is evident from history that man will by nature worship gods of his own making if left to himself. We do not know God or how to worship him by our own feelings or intellect. In fact, we do not find God; God finds us. We do not worship God out of the goodness of the human heart; God first cleanses us by washing us with the water and Word of Holy Baptism. Only then are we prepared to learn how to worship him rightly, and even then we revert at times to our own self-legislating inclinations. I recall a nearby congregation that announced it would no longer use bread and wine for the Lord's Supper; in keeping with the times, it now would substitute pizza and Coke as a way of speaking to today's generation. This should not be! From the beginning God has taught us who He is and how He is to be worshiped rightly for our salvation.

As a young man at the seminary I resented those teachers who said I had to learn to worship God rightly, implying that I had been worshiping God wrongly. It was only after some years in the parish ministry that it became clear to me that I was indeed more under the influence of my own piety (good feelings) than under the influence of the body of Christ and its worship through the ages. In the beginning of my parish ministry I tried, with sincerity and good intentions, to reinvent worship to make it relevant to my parishioners. Although what I created was still within the parameters of acceptability to the church, I was not hesitant to personally rewrite introits, collects, and creeds to express a piety shaped more by tastes than by the meaning of what God was doing in the Divine Service. It took the slow passage of time and the hammering away of God's Spirit to make clear that taste had little to do with worship. It is we who must change, and not the liturgy of the Divine Service. Liturgy may change over the centuries, but the change is in the matter of detail, not of substance. The words of Jesus take on new significance for those of us tempted to throw out or radically change the liturgy and remind us that, "He must become greater; I must become less" (John 3:30).

Partly under the influence of a culture that has breathed into us the breath of making worship acceptable as a way of increasing the market share of the church on a Sunday morning, and partly under the influence of sincere but short-sighted piety that equates the worship of God with feeling good about God, too many congregations today have given themselves over to the remaking of worship in their own image. I have been there, too, but I found that it is a dry and fruitless place that provides little more than camaraderie with like-minded people. It is not the way of worship once delivered to the saints where God leads us into His presence on His terms.

The contrast between ways of worshiping is not the issue of liturgy or no liturgy. There is no such thing as worship without liturgy, for liturgy is ritual, and human beings always follow ritual. Ritual, liturgy, is merely the habit of form. The only question is whether that ritual will be given us by God or made up by us according to our tastes. Liturgy conveys the essence and meaning of our worship of God. Worship is more than personal piety and personal expressions of faith. It is the experience of God's acting in our behalf so that we might act in His behalf in this world. Some years ago I was privileged to participate in the liturgy of foot washing on Maundy Thursday. I had been the vacancy pastor of a congregation that had followed the ancient custom of the pastor washing the feet of his parishioners (in this case a select, symbolic number of people who were brought to the chancel for this purpose). As I bathed the feet of each, I was humbled more than ever before. The meaning of this liturgy is to convey the vocation of our crucified Lord's ministry as handed down to His people. As Jesus bathed the feet of His disciples, He gave them a vocation to serve even as He had come to serve them. Thus a deeply significant ritual had recovered this vocation from the Lord. A congregation had demonstrated what words could not express. It was a ritual of the ancient church once lost and rediscovered, practiced by the church since New Testament times. The ritual is no mere hype to keep the interest of the audience. This was no feel-good experience associated with making the audience want to come again next week to see how the pastor would top this one. The ritual conveyed the command of Christ that as He came to serve, so we are all called to serve Christ in this world by being servants of one another.

The purpose of this book is not to speak about liturgy as an end in itself. The purpose has been to enlarge the understanding of the liturgy of the Divine Service as the way God gives healing to the soul on Sunday morning and throughout the week. The Divine Service is what it says of itself: It is a Divine Service by God to His people. God serves us the healing power of His absolution and feeds us His own healing Word and His own healing body and blood so that He might live in us and through us all our days.

We live in a culture that is increasingly dysfunctional. We are no longer certain how to define marriage and family. We hesitate to set limits by law to the freedom of some who pander to the lowest of human desires to express itself perversely without shame. We rush through every day as if being busy is the highest good. We have lost the ability to invest our lives in the safety of the elderly who have become the targets of scams and abuse by predators. We are a culture of people living with more stress, more activity, and more bodily ailments than ever. So overrun are we by the latest trends that we no longer hear God's calling: "Do not conform any longer to the pattern of this world, but be transformed by the renewing of your mind" (Romans 12:2).

The need for the healing of our lives at the core is crucial to our existence as a nation. Since it is only in public worship on a Sunday morning that people will have contact with God's self-revelation in Word and Sacraments, it is imperative that we consider the gift God gives in the Divine Service and not let it disappear into the marketplace of competing products. God chooses to speak to us as one body and, in that speaking, gives us Himself through His own body and blood. We need to be present to receive the healing that will save us now and forever. God gives us what we hardly know we need. In the liturgy of Holy Baptism in the Divine Service, we were marked with the sign of the cross on our foreheads and on our hearts to show that we are redeemed by Christ, the crucified. So we return to Him often in penitence and holy joy and sup with Him in the liturgy of Holy Communion. In so doing, we hear again the Gospel promise—"They will see His face, and His name will be on their foreheads" (Revelation 22:4).

NOTES

1. Gene Edward Veith, *The Spirituality of the Cross* (St. Louis, Mo.: Concordia Publishing House, 1999).

2. *EITHER/OR: A FRAGMENT OF LIFE* by Søren Kierkegaard, edited by Victor Eremita, abridged, translated and with an introduction and notes by Alastair Hannay (Penguin Classics, 1992) copyright © Alastair Hannay, 1992.

3. *The Voyage of the Dawn Treader* by C.S. Lewis, copyright © C.S. Lewis Pte. Ltd. 1952. Extract reprinted by permission.

4. *Lutheran Worship* (St. Louis, Mo.: Concordia Publishing House, 1982), p. 158.

5. *Lutheran Worship*, p. 158.

6. *Lutheran Worship*, p. 170.

7. The Small Catechism of Martin Luther.

8. See Luther's Small Catechism.

9. *Lutheran Worship*, p. 169.

10. *Lutheran Worship*, p. 146.

11. *The Magician's Nephew* by C.S. Lewis, copyright © C.S. Lewis Pte. Ltd. 1955. Extract reprinted by permission.

12. *Letters to Malcolm* by C.S. Lewis, copyright © C.S. Lewis Pte. Ltd. 1963, 1964. Extract reprinted by permission.

13. Augustine, *Confessions* (Oxford: Oxford University Press, 1991), p. 3.

14. Augustine, p. 218.

15. Augustine, p. 208.

16. *Lutheran Worship*, p. 159.

17. *Lutheran Worship*, p. 175.

18. *Lutheran Worship*, p. 67.

19. *Lutheran Worship*, p. 169.

20. *Lutheran Worship*, p. 146.

21. *Lutheran Worship*, pp. 170–171.

22. *Lutheran Worship*, p. 137.

23. Matthew Harrison, "The Church in the World," *For The Life of the World* 5 (July 2001): 14.

24. Reprinted from *Lutheran Book of Worship*, copyright © 1978, by permission of Augsburg Fortress.

25. Gene Edward Veith, *Postmodern Times: A Christian Guide to Contemporary Thought and Culture* (Wheaton, Ill.: Crossway Books, 1994), p. 54. Used by permission of Crossways Books, Wheaton, Illinois 60187

26. Aldous Huxley, *Brave New World* (New York: Harper Perrenial, 1932/1989).